SECOND EDITION

Charts
for Children

Print Awareness Activities
for Young Children

Judy Nyberg

D1364746

Good Year Books
Tucson, Arizona

Educational Standards

Charts for Children contains lessons and activities that reinforce and develop skills as defined by the International Reading Association and the National Council of Teachers of English as appropriate for students in PreK to Grade 1. These activities include early writing, reading, listening, and speaking skills. See www.goodyearbooks.com for information on how lessons correlate to specific standards.

Good Year Books

Our titles are available for most basic curriculum subjects plus many enrichment areas. For information on other Good Year Books and to place orders, contact your local bookseller or educational dealer, or visit our website at www.goodyearbooks.com. For a complete catalog, please contact:

Good Year Books
PO Box 91858
Tucson, AZ 85752-1858
www.goodyearbooks.com

Second Edition Cover Design:
 Gary Smith, Performance Design
Original Cover and Text Design:
 Meighan Depke
Cover and Title Page Illustrations:
 Brian Karas
Second Edition Text Design:
 Doug Goewey
Original Interior Drawings:
 Ruta Daugavietis
Additional Interior Drawings:
 Sean O'Neill

A GOOD YEAR BOOK™

Contents

Introduction

Stories and Activities

Using Stories to Provide Print-rich Experiences

". . . and Goldilocks never went uninvited into a house again.

The end."

". . . and the three billy goats lived happily ever after.

The end."

". . . so I will eat the bread. And she did, every last bite.

The end."

The End of the Story Is the Beginning of Activities

The well-loved story or favorite rhyme has been read and brought to its familiar conclusion. After a brief discussion, in which the young listeners relate their favorite parts of the story, they are often dismissed from the story rug and directed to their tables for a snack. Perhaps, after reading *The Little Red Hen,* they will feast on freshly baked rolls they have laboriously poked and shaped until the dough resembles hard little pebbles. The resplendent rolls will be served with delicious everyone-takes-a-turn-at-shaking-the-jar butter.

In a literacy-rich, print-rich early childhood classroom, the end of the story is, truly, just the beginning. It is the beginning of a series of literacy events—events and activities that incorporate authentic reading and writing; events that focus on the wonders and functions of print; events that support the philosophy that young children are readers and writers. In a print-rich classroom, the recipe for the rolls would probably be written out for all to see and read together. The experience of baking and eating the rolls would be talked about and documented in writing for all to read together. Perhaps the class might together write an invitation to the Little Red Hen. Would she like to see how they all helped to make the rolls? Children might suggest words describing the other animals in the story and watch as their teacher writes the words on a chart. Most likely they would then use those words in their own attempts at writing. Perhaps the class would compose a letter of inquiry to the local bakery. Could we please come and smell your delicious baking bread?

Charts for Children is a collection of activities for use following the telling of selected, familiar stories and rhymes. The activities focus on creating charts or visual displays in the classroom that provide reading, writing, and thinking opportunities for young children. The chart activities extend the stories into other curriculum areas, such as mathematics, social studies, or science. The well-loved stories and rhymes become the theme or package around which daily activities are developed. The major focus or intent of the activities is to provide opportunities for groups of children to see reading and writing modeled and to involve those groups in the reading and writing process.

The sample charts pictured in *Charts for Children* are adult-created. They are models of activities that can be carried out in your own classroom.

Literacy in the Early Childhood Setting

Current theories regarding how children learn to read and write have favorably affected the experiences offered young children when they enter the early childhood classroom. We know that young children come to school—preschool, kindergarten, or the primary grades—with all kinds of literacy history and experience. We know, for example, that children have been reading lots of environmental print, such as signs on the street and in the grocery store. We know that young children have been scribbling and drawing and writing, sometimes in sand, or on windows and walls, as well as on paper. We know that some young children have been read to for countless hours before they enter school. For other children, we know that the school setting provides the first opportunity to look at and investigate print and to begin to make meaning out of letters and words.

In a literacy-rich classroom, children are surrounded with print and their days are filled with activities that invite them to use and interact with that print. Children are encouraged to "pretend," or attempt, to read and to write. They are beginning readers and writers who are striving to make sense out of print. Thus the early childhood teacher's responsibility is not to get children *ready* to read and write; but it is to get them reading and writing—in their own way. Given opportunities for practice with print, children will gradually move from "pretend" or approximate reading and writing to conventional or "adult like" reading and writing.

Of equal importance is the belief that all attempts at reading and writing are valued and honored. Mistakes are made and approximations are respected. Trying on the *behaviors* of readers and writers is an essential part of the process of becoming real readers and writers.

Given this understanding, the early childhood teacher is charged with providing a visually exciting environment where opportunities for discovery of and practice with print abound. Early childhood teachers have long known the inherent value of reading to children. They also understand that good children's literature can become the springboard for developing exciting curricula for the day or week. When developing a theme or topic that springs from literature, the classroom can become alive with opportunities for oral and written language development. *Charts for Children* provides ideas and activities centering on twelve well-loved stories and rhymes. The suggested activities can, however, easily be transferred to literature that goes beyond the traditional favorites presented in this volume.

The challenge is to let your imagination run wild as you dream up story-related activities. What would the children enjoy doing? What is relevant to their experience? How can I expand their thinking and imagining? What activities will help them focus on print? What activities reflect authentic reading and writing?

We've Heard These Stories Before

There are, of course, reasons why stories such as *The Three Little Pigs* or rhymes such as "The Three Little Kittens" have endured and continue to be passed down from generation to generation. The traditional tales, with their different-time, far-away settings, let children see how less-than-threatening characters resolve conflicts. The tales give children an understanding of the world even as they transport them far away from their own circumstances, giving them a glimpse of the universality of human problems. Of course, young children are not aware that Goldilocks is a universal example of bad manners and lack of common sense as she enters the bears' house uninvited. Rather, they are swept up with Goldilocks in the unfolding drama.

The same old stories should be heard again and again because they provide pure pleasure for children. Young children are very interested in folk tales. They are interested because they believe. They believe in magic and the presence of magic in their own lives. They believe that animals can think and talk. And they believe in a sense of justice that is often apparent in folk tales. The stories allow children to reexamine familiar themes and plots while providing examples for their own imaginations and story creating. Children derive a great deal of satisfaction from the familiar tales that give them a sense of control as they say, "I know that one!"

Extend the Story

The activities presented in *Charts for Children* reflect a process that begins with story selection. As you choose stories and activities for your children, consider children's past story experiences, their background knowledge, and their interests. Conversation and background-building to heighten interest and to familiarize children with new vocabulary and concepts always precedes successful story reading or telling.

Read It Again and Again

Read the story or rhyme for pure enjoyment and then read it again and again. Revisit the same book often. Read variations of the story so that children can compare texts and illustrations. You might start with the Grimm's version of *Little Red Riding Hood*, for example, and then read Ed Young's story of *Lon Po Po*, a Chinese tale.

Once children are very familiar with the story and know the ending well, they are ready to begin doing the extension activities.

Make a Web of Concepts to Develop from the Story

All stories are rich with concepts that can be fully developed into activities and literacy events across the curriculum. You might begin by making a web of words or topics that are related to a story. Narrow the choices down to one or two topics that you think children would most like to explore. Constructing word webs often helps us, as adults, think about how stories present concepts to young learners—concepts we sometimes take for granted. The following word web illustrates some topic possibilities for *Little Red Riding Hood*.

Create Language Experience Activities

Inviting children to become involved in the writing process by creating language experience charts has long been a popular early childhood activity. As children talk about and summarize a shared experience, they incorporate concepts and make them their own.

Language experience activities can take many forms. Your language experience activity for the day might be talking about Peter Rabbit's devastating experience in the garden, for example, and then writing a class letter to Peter. On another day, children might contribute to a chart by telling how they made peanut-butter-and-jelly sandwiches. As you record the words and sentences children create and offer, you model writing. As you read the charts together, you provide opportunities for children to use conventions of print, to understand the concept of word, and to build their sight vocabularies. As the completed charts are displayed around the classroom, they become tools for children's independent reading. "Look! I know what this says!" The charts can be read and savored again and again.

It is important to acknowledge that language experience activities or charts are only *one* piece of the total reading-writing process that young children should experience. The beauty of language experience activities is in the opportunity to model reading and writing. The activity crosses all curriculum areas as various topics and charts are conceived.

We know that children learn to read and write by doing just that—by reading and writing. Thus children need to have experiences that go beyond the modeling process and group-dictated or group-created charts. They need many opportunities to use a variety of materials, encouraging writing and creating on their own. They need time each day to read books and to explore print independently. The activities suggested in *Charts for Children* focus on providing print activities for the entire class or group. As such, they are but only one print-awareness activity available in a literacy-rich classroom.

Involve Children

The *Charts for Children* activities promote children's participation as charts are created. Children are not just observers, they are doers. When creating group charts or stories, try to involve all children in the process so that each child takes ownership of the end product. Children can not only contribute to the text by negotiating what is written and by providing specific words or sentences, but also by decorating or elaborating the chart with drawings or other art pieces, which involves deciding where each of their contributions should be positioned on the chart. When a group works together to create charts and murals, each product takes on its own life and identity, reflecting in this case the children in your classroom.

Creating a chart or group-dictated story encourages lots of oral language learning and conversation before the finalized version is written down. Children's thinking becomes public. This conversation and collective offering of ideas, this oral problem-solving, allows children to try out their thoughts on the group and see that their contributions are honored. Meaning is enhanced as children build on the understandings of one another.

When a chart is completed, read the words or sentences on the chart to model the reading process, and then encourage children to read with you. Point to each word as you read so that children can see and hear the one-to-one correspondence of the spoken to written word. Read the text again and again so that it becomes very familiar to children. And remember, if you think that children are memorizing the words, not really reading them, that's great! It's the *behaviors* of reading that are so important for beginning readers.

The imitation of the act of reading is a natural first step. Read and revisit the text as a group for several days. Encourage children to "read the walls," either as an individual or as a partner activity.

Creating Independent Response Activities

You can make the charts more interactive by providing daily challenges for children based on the charts you've displayed around the room. Invite children to investigate concepts, solve problems, take polls, or answer questions in writing. If children are not yet reading, read the Take Another Look activity or question for them at the beginning of the day. Talk about the directions and possible responses. Then invite them to respond to the activity at their leisure sometime during the day. If you take a poll or record written responses, summarize the results at the end of the day.

Dear Red Ridinghood,

You'd better listen to your mother next time. Stay on the path. Don't talk to wolves.

Your friends in Mrs. Classen's Class

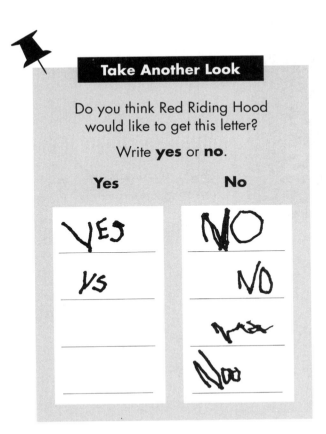

Take Another Look

Do you think Red Riding Hood would like to get this letter?

Write **yes** or **no**.

Yes	No

Literacy Across the Curriculum

Children will eagerly anticipate each day's opportunity for personal response. "I wonder what surprise will be waiting for us today?"

As you plan your program, consider how you can turn all areas of the curriculum into literacy events. Read the words and labels on graphs and number charts, record science-related observations, write down steps in a process, and make up recipes for a healthy breakfast. Reading and writing don't stop when science time or math time begins.

The Stories and Rhymes in *Charts for Children*

You'll find suggested activities for the twelve stories and rhymes listed. Use them in your program as you explore themes and topics. Then, expand on your own favorite stories and rhymes by creating additional charts, providing new reading, writing, and thinking experiences for young children.

Goldilocks and the Three Bears

The Three Little Pigs

The Gingerbread Man

The Three Little Kittens

The Tortoise and the Hare

Henny Penny

The Three Billy Goats Gruff

Peter Rabbit

The Little Red Hen

Stone Soup

Five Little Monkeys

Humpty Dumpty

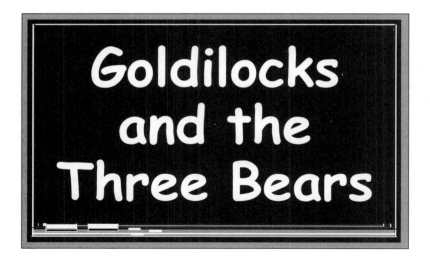

See another activity for this story on page 177.

Books to Read

Marshall, James. *Goldilocks and the Three Bears.* (Dial, 1991).

Stevens, Janet. *Goldilocks and the Three Bears.* (Holiday House, 1986).

Barton, Byron. *The Three Bears.* (Harper, 1991).

Tolhurst, Marilyn. *Somebody and the Three Blairs.* (Orchard, 1991).

About the Story

All children seem to love the story of Goldilocks. When they first encounter the story, young children don't appear to mind that Goldilocks enters the three bears' house uninvited. They don't appear to be outraged by her eating up all the porridge or by her breaking Baby Bear's chair. They understand that Goldilocks is hungry, so it seems natural that she would help herself to the bears' food. Similarly, children often try out furniture in a new setting, so it seems perfectly normal that Goldilocks would flop down in the bears' chairs. It is only when the sleeping Goldilocks is discovered by the bears that children begin to realize that the central character is in big trouble. Up until this point, young listeners usually have been marveling at bears who cook and eat and they delight in the predictability of the story elements that come in threes. Only after the story has been enjoyed again and again are young listeners ready to consider Goldilocks's inappropriate behaviors.

This story provides a perfect background for exploring breakfast foods and for finding out about real bears, among other things.

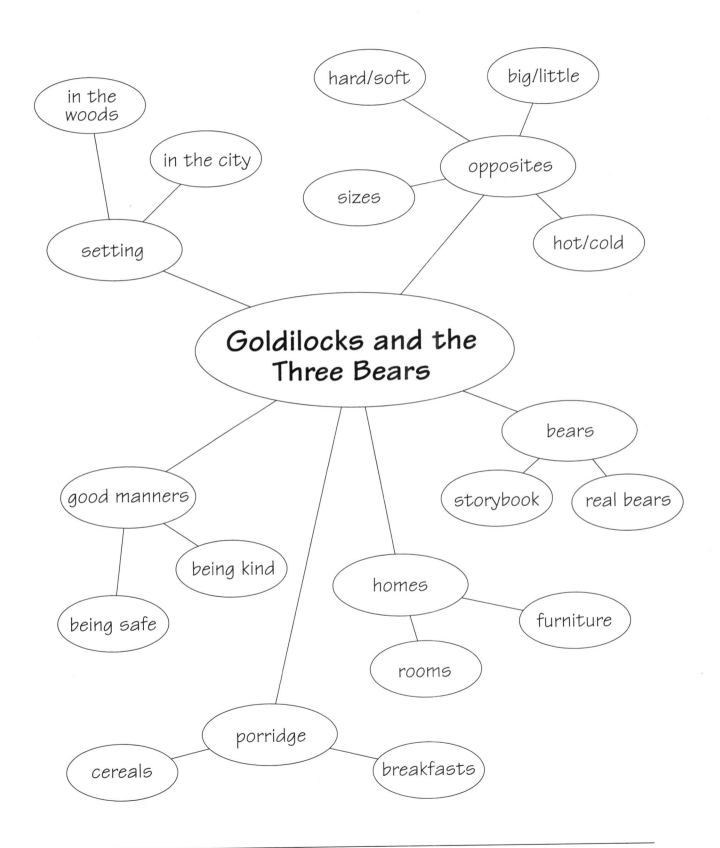

Bowls for the Bears

- Talk about the objects mentioned in the story—the big, middle-sized, and little bowls, chairs, and beds. Point out the objects in the illustrations that accompany the story you have read.

- Show children examples of objects that come in various sizes, such as balls, dolls, or T-shirts. Invite them to decide which objects would be used by Papa, Mama, or Baby Bear.

- Display the "Bowls for the Bears" chart. Read the chart with children, explaining what they are to do.

- Demonstrate the process by making a big, a middle-sized, and a little construction-paper bowl. Decorate the bowls and label with the characters' names.

- Attach the bowls to the appropriate columns and then invite each child to make a bowl for his or her favorite bear.

- After children have attached their bowls to the chart, confirm as a group that the sizes are appropriate and count the total number of bowls in each column.

Take Another Look

Who's your favorite bear?

Mark an X under its name.

Papa Bear	Mama Bear	Baby Bear

Bowls for the Bears

Make a bowl for Papa, Mama, or Baby Bear.

Is your bowl big, middle-sized, or little?

Put your bowl in the correct column.

Our Favorite Cereals

- If possible, take a field trip to a grocery store to explore the breakfast cereals display.

- Encourage children to talk about cereals they like to eat. Help them use describing words as they tell why they like certain cereals.

- Invite children to bring from home empty cereal boxes. Display these in the classroom, or use them in the dramatic play grocery store area.

- Read the type on the cereal boxes. Talk about the ingredients and the nutritional qualities, such as vitamins and minerals.

- Prepare a "Favorite Cereals" chart similar to the example shown. Have children observe as you write the words on the chart. Underline and talk about the title of the chart. Point out the words *hot* and *cold*.

- As children name their favorite cereals, have them tell you whether you should write the name of the cereal under *hot* or *cold*.

- Distribute squares of construction paper and invite children to draw boxes of their favorite cereals. Remind them to include the cereal names on their boxes.

- Have each child decide where to attach his or her box on the chart.

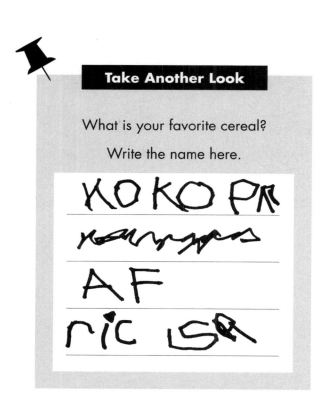

Take Another Look

What is your favorite cereal?

Write the name here.

Our Favorite Cereals

Is your favorite
cereal cold or is it hot?

Cold   Oat Flakies

            CoCo Crunch

            Corn Squares

Hot   Oatmeal

            Creamy Wheat

A New Story Ending

- Read several versions of the story and compare the story endings. Encourage children to think about how Goldilocks must have felt when she was awakened by the bears and how surprised the bears must have been to find her sleeping in their house.

- Take a class vote to determine if children are happy with the way the story ended. Do they think Goldilocks should have gotten away? Should she have apologized to the bears? Perhaps she should have offered to make the bed or to bring the bears some breakfast.

- After discussing several possibilities for a different story ending, invite children to contribute to writing a new ending. Encourage children to talk together—to negotiate how the story is to be written—before you record individual sentences on a story chart.

- As you add each sentence, reread the chart from the beginning.

- Make the chart available in the writing center and invite children to draw their own Goldilocks on the chart or to attach construction-paper versions.

Take Another Look

Do you like this story ending better?

Make a check mark.

Yes	No

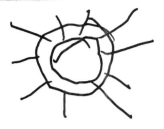

A New Story Ending

Goldilocks woke up fast. She was scared of the bears. She said she was sorry about coming into the house. Papa Bear said, "Let's have lunch." So they all had pizza. And they were friends forever.

How We Made Porridge

- Invite conversation about children's experiences with eating and enjoying hot cereals. Recall that in the story, the Three Bears had to take a walk while their cereal cooled a little.

- Provide a box of hot cereal mix or instant hot cereal. (If you want to provide a different tasting experience, provide a thick pea soup for children to sample.) Read the name of the cereal and other words on the box for children.

- Follow the directions for making the cereal, inviting children to become part of the process by measuring and stirring. Talk about each step in the process as you prepare the cereal.

- Provide milk and various toppings, such as butter, brown sugar, berries, or jams.

- On the following day, recall with children each step in the process and then record a simplified version on a chart similar to the one shown.

- Have children sign their names on the chart, since they all helped to cook the porridge. For another writing experience, encourage them to write out their own recipes.

Take Another Look

Vote for your favorite topping.

Write your name under the one you like the best.

Berries	Butter	Sugar
JASON	OO	HASSIN
YU		PETER
		Sharr

JASON

Tory

How We Made Porridge

Rosi

1. Take 1 envelope of cereal out of the box.

2. Put the cereal in a bowl.

Lilly

3. Add 3/4 cup hot water.

4. Stir it up.

Ramon

5. Add some milk.

Kwan

6. Let it cool before you eat it.

Add your favorite topping.

berries

brown sugar

butter

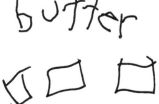
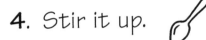

What Real Bears Do

- The concept of what is real and what is pretend in stories is a difficult one for children to understand. Even in real life, young children sometimes do not differentiate between the two. While we do not want to disturb children's sense of wonder and active imaginations, we can clarify for children that story animals often talk and wear clothing, whereas real animals do not.

- After reading *Goldilocks and the Three Bears,* talk about the bears in the story and what they do.

- Encourage children to bring teddy bears from home to reinforce the concept of pretend bears and real bears.

- Ask children to tell what they know about real bears.

- Provide picture books about bears, such as *A New True Book—Bears* by Mark Rosenthal (Childrens Press, 1983). Discuss some of the essential facts learned about bears in nature.

- Prepare the chart, writing *What real bears do* and *What story bears do.* Read the words for children and then invite them to complete the chart with you, sharing facts they know.

- Encourage children to look at the picture books and then make their own bears to decorate the chart.

Take Another Look

Do you have a teddy bear at home?

Write the name here.

What Real Bears Do	What Story Bears Do
They live in the woods.	They make breakfast.
Some are big.	Story bears talk.
Bears have fur.	They wear clothes.
They eat fish.	They sleep in beds.
They sleep in the winter.	

B Is for Bear!

- Use the story to explore the letter *Bb*. Locate the letter several times in the text, using the words *baby* and *bear.*

- Emphasize the words as you say them, helping children hear the b sound.

- Identify objects in the classroom that begin with the letter *b,* such as book, barrette, bracelet, and ball.

- List children's names that begin with the letter *B.*

- Make a list of good names for Baby Bear that begin with the letter *B.*

- Invite children to contribute *b* words to the chart. As you write the words, underline the letter *b,* or write the letter in a different color to make it more visible.

- Invite children to illustrate the words they suggested.

- Have children say the words with you many times.

- Encourage children to make their own *B* books at the writing table, transferring the words from the chart to their own books and adding new *b* words.

Take Another Look

Do you know anyone whose name begins with the letter *B*?

Write that person's name here.

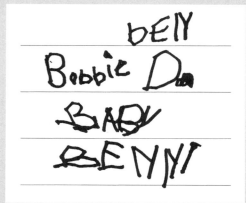

B Is for Bear!

<u>B</u> is a wonderful letter.

What other words begin with <u>Bb</u>?

<u>b</u>all

<u>b</u>aby

<u>b</u>utter

<u>b</u>rown

<u>b</u>ell

<u>b</u>utton

<u>b</u>icycle

<u>B</u>obby

<u>b</u>arrette

<u>b</u>ook

The Three Little Pigs

See another activity for this story on page 177.

Books to Read

Claverie, Jean. *The Three Little Pigs.* (North-South, 1989).

Marshall, James. *The Three Little Pigs.* (Dial, 1989).

Rounds, Glen. *The Three Little Pigs.* (Holiday House, 1992).

Scieszka, Jon. *The True Story of the Three Little Pigs.* (Viking, 1989).

About the Story

"Little pig, little pig, let me come in."
"Not by the hair of my chinny chin chin."
"Then I'll huff and I'll puff and I'll blow your house in."

These famous, predictable refrains from the story about three little pigs hold enchantment for young children who are just a little bit terrified of the Big Bad Wolf. Children can quickly make sense of and anticipate the structure of the story as each of the three pigs finds material to build a house and then deals with the threat of the wolf. The predictable refrains of the characters and the repeated patterns of the story events invite children's interaction. Just as children enjoy repeating

Goldilocks's refrain ". . . too hard . . . too soft . . . just right!" they delight in the repetition of the wolf's and pigs' lines, quickly committing them to memory.

Young listeners will appreciate simplified versions of the story, while more experienced listeners will enjoy versions of Joseph Jacobs's original story, which includes meetings with the wolf in a butter churn and at an apple orchard.

The story sets the scene for exploring neighborhoods, and for finding out about real pigs, among other things.

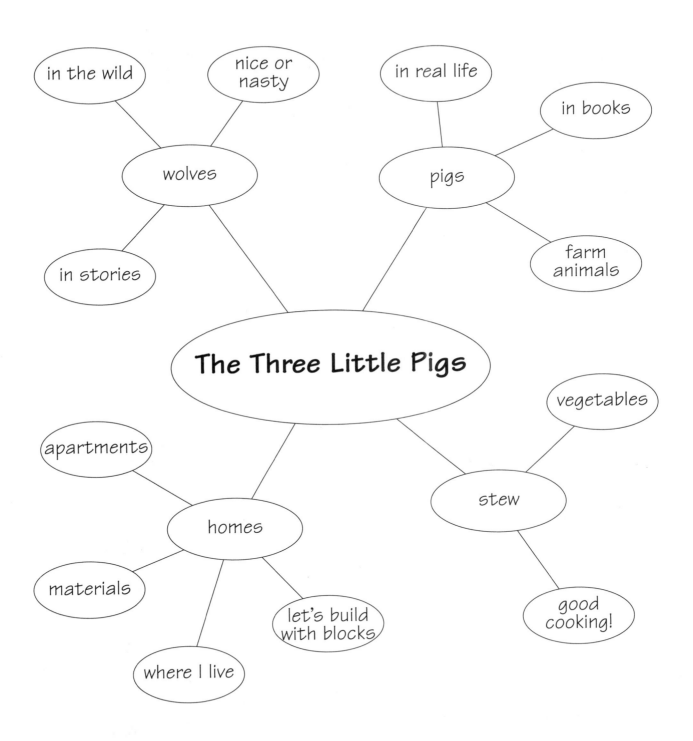

Homes in Our Neighborhood

- Explore the neighborhood around the school with children. Help them observe the sizes, shapes, and colors of the houses and apartment buildings.

- After returning to the classroom, recall with children what they saw. You might want to list adjectives children use in describing what they saw.

- Encourage conversation and comment from all children and then compose a group-dictated story that tells about the experience.

- As you add each new sentence, reread the story in its entirety.

- Invite children to decorate the chart with drawings of houses and apartment buildings or by making these out of construction paper.

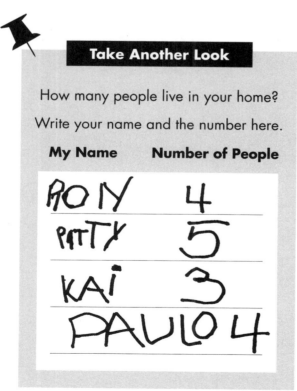

Take Another Look

How many people live in your home?

Write your name and the number here.

My Name	Number of People
ROIY	4
PATTY	5
KAI	3
PAULO	4

Take Another Look

Do you know your name and address?

Write your name and the address here.

My Name	My Address
ROSA	
551 KIRM	
ANKERN	
675 SOMTH	

Homes in Our Neighborhood

We took a walk. We saw lots of houses. Some houses were big.

We saw where Darnell lives. He sure lives in a big house!

Come into My Home

- Invite children to name and describe the rooms in their own homes.

- Show pictures of furnishings and have children name and describe some of the furnishings in their own homes.

- Provide furniture and home furnishing catalogs. Invite children to cut out pictures of furnishings with which they are familiar.

- Create an outline of a house or apartment on a piece of chart paper. Let children decide which rooms they will identify and furnish on the chart.

- Then have children contribute to the list of items found in each room.

- Have children attach catalog pictures to each item or draw their own versions of the objects.

Take Another Look

What is your favorite room in your house or apartment?

Write the name of the room and your name here.

Room   **My Name**

Come into my home.
This is what you will find.

The living room

a television

chairs

a couch

a rug

My bedroom

my bed

a lamp

my books

blankets

my toys

The kitchen

a stove

dishes

a table

chairs

a sink

The bathroom

my toothbrush

towels

our bathtub

a sink

a toilet

A Map of Our Neighborhood

- Take a walk around the school with children. Point out streets and identifying buildings.

- In class, name and list some of the things you saw and encourage conversation about how children identify places around the school.

- Show examples of maps and explain their purpose.

- Suggest drawing a map of your neighborhood. Invite children to decide how the map will be made. Will everyone take turns drawing various places or do the children want you to draw the map as they describe the neighborhood to you?

- Encourage children to color in the map.

Take Another Look

How many homes do you see on the map? Count them and write the number and your name here.

My Name   Number of Homes

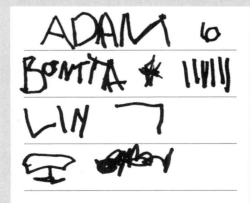

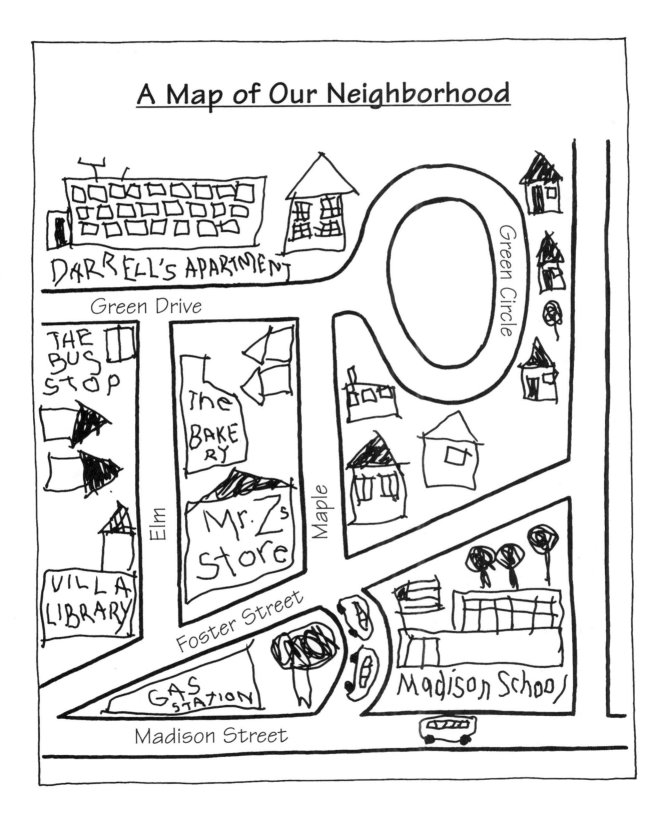

A Map of Our Neighborhood

DARRELL'S APARTMENT

Green Drive

Green Circle

THE BUS STOP

Elm

The BAKERY

Mr. Z's Store

Maple

VILLA LIBRARY

Foster Street

GAS STATION

Madison School

Madison Street

How Do You Go to School?

- Discuss the various ways children get to school.

- Describe how you yourself get to school each day.

- Prepare a graph that includes simple diagrams of a bus, a car, or a child walking that children can identify.

- Give each child a square of paper that will fit in a space on the graph. Have children draw pictures of their own modes of transportation and attach them to the graph.

- Count and write the totals on the graph.

Take Another Look

What did you see on your way to school?

Write a story or draw a picture.

How Do You Go to School?

I walk.	Denise	Ian	Rosa	Paul	4
I ride the bus.	Jason	Camilla	Ramon	Jesse	4
I ride my bike.	Rachel	Darrel			2
I ride in a car.	Sylvia				1

All About Pigs

- Encourage children to think about what the three pigs did in the story. Do pigs really say goodbye to their mothers? Do pigs really build houses?

- Invite children to tell you what they know about real pigs.

- Create a KWL chart on a piece of paper. Explain that in the first column you will write what children KNOW about real pigs. In the second column you will write what children WANT TO KNOW, and in the last column you will write new things that they have LEARNED about pigs after they read about them.

- Fill in the first two columns. Then read picture books about real pigs, such as *Farm Animal Stories—Pig* by Angela Royston (Warwick Press, 1990) or *Farm Noises* by Jane Miller (Simon and Schuster, 1989). Have children help you fill in the third column.

- Provide construction paper so that children can create their own pigs and decorate the chart.

Take Another Look

Give this little pig a good name.

Be sure the name starts with the letter *P*.

All About Pigs

What We Know	What We Want to Know	What We Learned
Pigs are pink. Pigs say "oink." Pigs love mud. Pigs have curly tails.	Are there other colors? How many babies do pigs have? What do pigs really eat?	Pigs cool off in the mud. Today, most pigs live in barns. Some paint brushes are made of pig hair.

Pig Poetry

- Prepare a chart similar to the one shown.

- Read the poem with children several times, pointing out and enjoying the rhyming words *pig/jig* and *hog/jog.*

- Have children join in saying the poem with you and encourage them to clap to the rhythm of the poem as you say the words together.

- Then, write the first two lines of a new nonsense poem, inviting children to provide the rhyming words. (Remember, the poems do not have to make sense. The idea is to give children experience with rhyming words—an important prereading or early-reading concept. Listening to and coming up with rhyming words encourages children to play with language. This language play is crucial to their literacy development.)

Take Another Look

Think of a word that rhymes with the words you see.

Write it down.

hat	**pig**
Cat	G
SAt	pig
Pat	WG

Animal Poems

To market, to market to buy a fat <u>pig.</u>

Home again, home again, jiggety <u>jig.</u>

To market, to market to buy a fat <u>hog.</u>

Home again, home again, jiggety <u>jog.</u>

To market, to market to buy a fat <u>duck.</u>

Home again, home again, clickety <u>cluck.</u>

To market, to market to buy a fat <u>cow.</u>

Home again, home again <u>bow wow wow.</u>

See another activity for this story on page 177.

Books to Read

Galdone, Paul. *The Gingerbread Boy.* (Seabury, 1975).

Cook, Scott. *The Gingerbread Boy.* (Knopf, 1987).

Kimmel, Eric. *The Gingerbread Man.* (Holiday House, 1993).

About the Story

Run, run, as fast as you can. You can't catch me. I'm the Gingerbread Man.

This refrain is a favorite of children as they come to identify with the seemingly unbelievable gingerbread cookie who springs to life from the pan. The predictability and repetition of the story pattern as the Gingerbread Man encounters and runs from various farm animals allows young listeners to quickly participate in the telling of the story. The fate of the Gingerbread Man is to be eaten by the crafty fox who volunteers to carry the cookie on his back across the river. Several versions of the tale, such as Eric Kimmel's version mentioned above, include ending text that makes readers aware that cookies are meant to be eaten and it's all just pretend. Children may appreciate some clarifying conversation, so that they are not frightened by the fact that the main character gets gobbled up by the fox.

This story, like most traditional tales, has just the right balance of merriness and suspense to delight and capture the interest of the listener.

The story provides opportunities to extend concepts about farm animals, about the five basic senses, and, of course, about cookie baking, among other things.

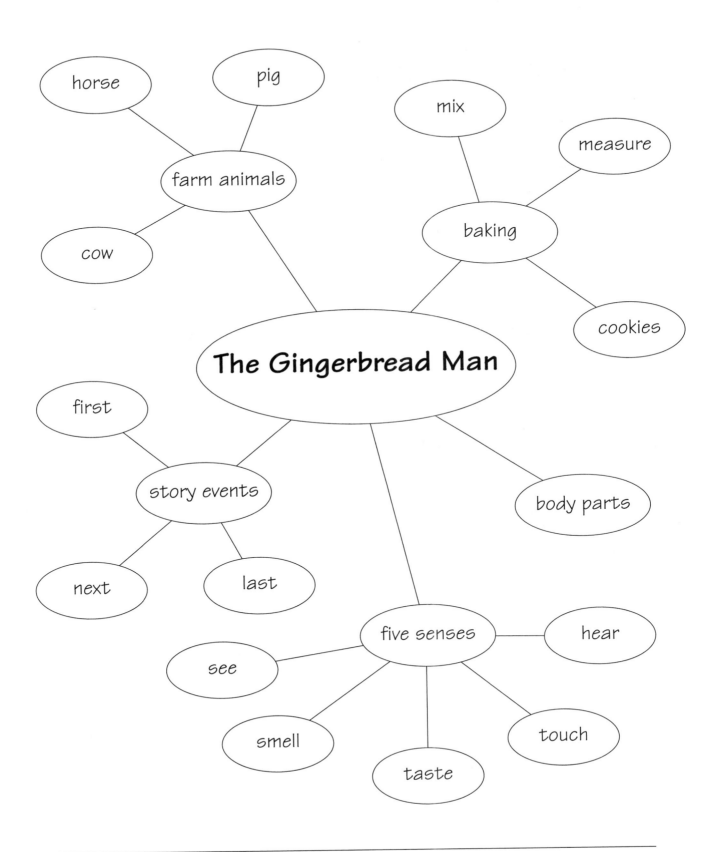

Where Do We Find Animals?

- Recall the animals named in the story and decide together that the animals named—horse, pig, cow— lived on a farm. Refer to the story illustrations.

- Familiarize children with other books showing animals that live on farms, such as *The Big Red Barn* by Margaret Wise Brown (HarperCollins, 1989), and animals that live in zoos, such as *Zoos* by Miriam Moss (Bookwright Press, 1987).

- Prepare a chart with the title of the activity and a simple drawing suggesting a farm and a zoo.

- Read the words with children and then invite them to name animals found in each location.

- Remember to reread the names as the list continues to grow.

- Encourage children to create pictures of the animals they suggested and attach them to the chart.

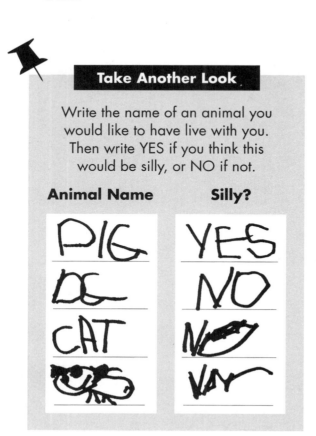

Take Another Look

Write the name of an animal you would like to have live with you. Then write YES if you think this would be silly, or NO if not.

Animal Name   **Silly?**

PIG   YES

DG   NO

CAT   NO

Do We Find Animals

On the Farm?	In the Zoo?
horse	zebra
pig	elephant
cow	seal
rooster	bear

A Recipe for Gingerbread Men

- Invite children to help you prepare a recipe for gingerbread cookies. When children are involved in doing the activity, instead of just watching you do it, they will remember the experience.

- Be sure children participate in rolling out the cookie dough and cutting out the cookie shapes.

- As children take part in the process, draw their attention to using their senses of sight, smell, touch, and taste.

- After the cookies have been decorated and eaten, help children recall the steps involved and record the experience as children take turns dictating to you.

- Invite children to decorate the chart by drawing their own Gingerbread Men, or by tracing a pattern for them to follow.

Take Another Look

How did you like the gingerbread cookies? Make an X.

I think our gingerbread men tasted

Yummy	Not so Yummy

Gingerbread Men

1. Roll the dough flat.

2. Use the cookie cutter.

3. Put on the pan and bake.

4. Decorate with candy and frosting and raisins.

They are good!
Smell them baking!

Write a Letter

- After rereading the story, invite children to think about how the man and the woman in the story must have felt when the Gingerbread Man jumped up and started to run away.

- Invite children to take turns role-playing the beginning of the story, taking the parts of the man and woman and the Gingerbread Man.

- Then discuss how the man and woman could be cheered up. What could the class do that would be nice? Send a card? a letter? pictures?

- Carry out children's suggestions, such as recording a class-dictated letter or an invitation to the man and woman.

- Expand on the concept by talking about nice things we can do for people to help them feel better.

- Invite children to illustrate the chart with story events.

Take Another Look

Make a pretend plate of your favorite cookies. Use a paper plate and construction paper.

How many cookies are on your plate today?

Dear Mr. and Mrs. Farmer,

We are sorry that your Gingerbread Man got away.

If you want to see some boys and girls, come visit us. We are in Mrs. King's Kindergarten at Ellis St. School.

Here are pictures about your story.

Love,
Mrs. King's Kindergarten

That's Tasty

- Involve children in a discussion about foods that are their favorites and those that are not as well liked.

- If possible, have a tasting party of foods that will be rated on a chart.

- Prepare a chart listing the names of foods to be rated and the rating scale of GREAT, GOOD, and OK.

- Have children put a circle, dot, or check in the appropriate columns to indicate their ratings. Which food has the most GREATs?

Take Another Look

On your own paper, make a list of things you want to buy at the grocery store.

Are the foods on your list healthy?

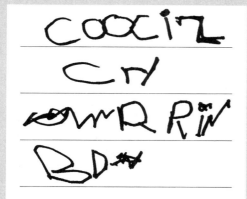

That's Tasty

Food	Great!	Good	OK
pizza			
cereal			
milk			
rice			
peanut butter			
apples			
soup			
hamburgers			

Cookies—We Love Them

- Invite children to a cookie-tasting party. Have them compare the various flavors and textures of several kinds of cookies.

- As children sample the cookies, help them use describing words to express what they are tasting and why they like it.

- Prepare a chart and have children record their favorite cookies by writing their names in the appropriate column.

Take Another Look

On a piece of paper, write your own recipe for cookies you would like to bake.

How many things go into your cookies?

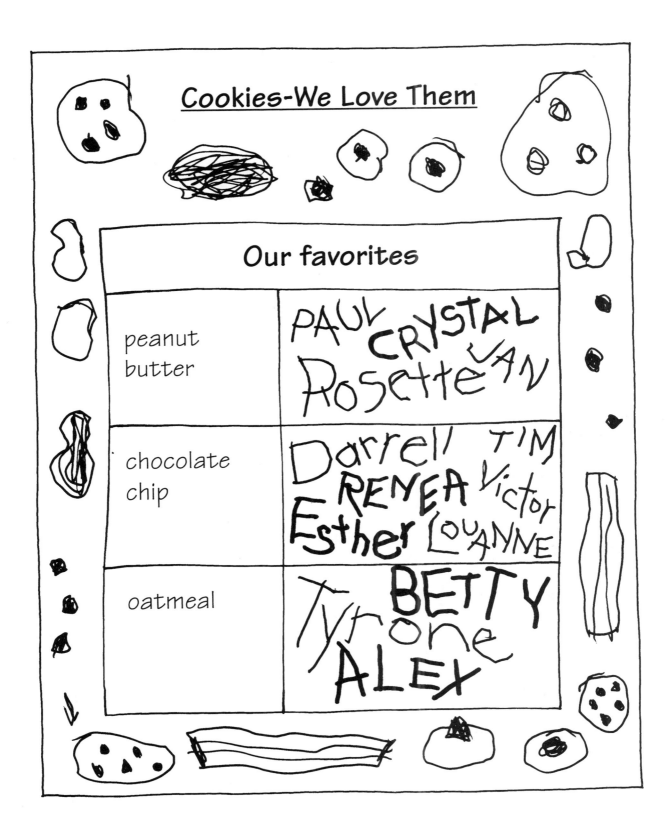

Cookies-We Love Them

Our favorites

peanut butter	PAUL CRYSTAL Rosette VAN
chocolate chip	Darrell TIM RENEA Victor Esther LOUANNE
oatmeal	BETTY Tyrone ALEX

Our Five Senses

- The concept of using the five senses can be rather abstract for young children. Activities explaining the concept should be concrete and real. Children need to hear sounds, feel objects and textures, and smell odors. Just talking about the senses by using pictures of objects makes the concept less tangible.

- Give children thinking time as you introduce the chart. Encourage them to think about things they have seen, heard, smelled, touched, or tasted that day.

- Invite them to contribute drawings or objects made from construction paper. Have children label their artwork or label it for them.

- Confirm that the drawings or objects are in the appropriate rows as you discuss the chart.

Take Another Look

Write the name of a food you ate today.

Your Name	The Food

Our Five Senses

We See	flower MOM rainboz (rainbow) (sun)
We Hear	(speaker) (dog) clok (clock)
We Smell	cookies (tulip) sampu (shampoo)
We Taste	cookez pizza org
We Touch	(cat) water

The Three Little Kittens

See more activities for this story on page 177.

Three little kittens, they lost their mittens,
And they began to cry,
Oh, Mother dear, we sadly fear
Our mittens we have lost.
What! Lost your mittens, you naughty kittens
Then you shall have no pie.
Mee-ow, mee-ow, mee-ow.
No, you shall have no pie.

The three little kittens, they found their mittens,
And they began to cry,
Oh, Mother dear, see here, see here,
Our mittens we have found.
Put on your mittens, you silly kittens,
And you shall have some pie.
Purr-r, purr-r, purr-r,
Oh, let us have some pie.

Books to Read

Butterworth, Nick. *Nick Butterworth's Book of Nursery Rhymes.* (Viking, 1990).

Livermore, Elaine. *Three Little Kittens Lost Their Mittens.* (Houghton, 1979).

Lobel, Arnold. *The Random House Book of Mother Goose.* (Random House, 1986).

About the Poem

This poem is such fun because it tells a story that young children understand. Envisioning kittens wearing mittens is funny, and losing them is something most children have experienced at some time.

The poem invites us to discover berries, fruits, and pies. It also provides a great opportunity to talk about rhyming words. Write the poem on a large piece of paper so that children can see it as you read the words.

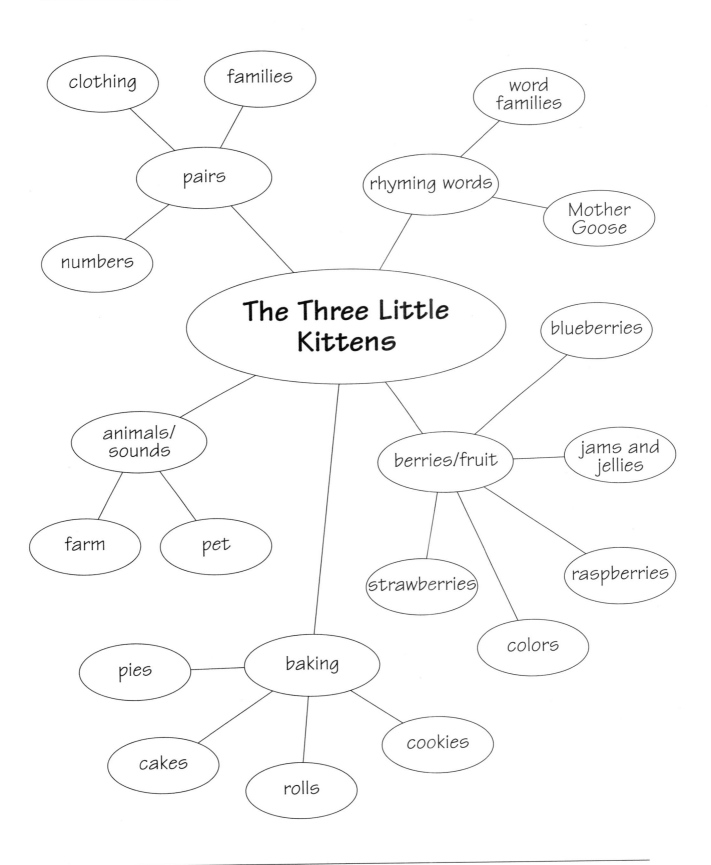

Find a Pair of Mittens

- Discuss the concept of pairs, showing children objects that come in pairs, such as shoes, socks, gloves, and mittens. If children are curious, explore why eyeglasses and jeans are called pairs.

- Make a left and a right mitten pattern on various colors of construction paper.

- Invite children to choose their own color paper, and cut out and decorate their own pair of mittens.

- When the mittens are completed, have children sit in a large circle on the floor. Mix up the pairs of mittens, placing them all on the floor inside the circle. Invite children to take turns finding the pairs they made.

- Explain to children that they are going to glue their mittens onto a large piece of paper to create a pairs game. Help them choose places for their mittens so that their left and right mittens are not too close together.

- When the game chart is completed, have children take turns finding and pointing out pairs.

Take Another Look

What color are your mittens?

Write your name and the color here.

My Name	Color
BRAD	BUE
TRON	Red
xessie	RED
RAFF	

Find a Pair of Mittens

A Recipe for "Little Pies"

- Prepare pie dough.

- Write simple directions for making pies or turnovers on a piece of chart paper.

- Read each step with children, pointing to the words as you read.

- Demonstrate the process as you read the steps again and follow the directions.

- Invite children to take turns making their own pies.

- Give each child a duplicated copy of the recipe to take home, or invite them to write their own recipes.

Take Another Look

What is your favorite kind of pie?

Write the name of the pie here.

A Recipe for

"Little Pies"

1. Roll out the pie dough.

2. Cut around a plate to make a dough circle.

3. Put berry jam on one side of the circle.

4. Fold the other side over.

5. Pinch the edges together.

6. Sprinkle sugar on top.

7. Bake until brown.

Fruit We Love the Best

- Ask each child to bring a piece of fruit to class for a fruit-tasting party.

- Have children help prepare the fruits by making them into bite-sized pieces.

- Give each child a toothpick. Invite children to sample pieces, asking them to think about each kind of fruit as they taste it. Talk about the flavors and textures. Is it juicy? Is it soft?

- Create a chart listing the names of fruits and make a sample construction-paper fruit to demonstrate what children will be doing.

- Draw children's attention to the size of the spaces on the chart; then invite them to choose their own favorite fruit, create one out of construction paper and attach it to the chart.

- Total the rows on the chart.

Take Another Look

Did you eat a fruit yesterday?

Was it at breakfast, lunch, or dinner?

Write your name and make an X.

Name	Breakfast	Lunch	Dinner
SONIA	X		
RObERt	X		

Fruit We Love the Best

apples								4
strawberries								3
bananas								5
oranges								3
blueberries								

Advice Column

- Talk about advice columns in newspapers. Show a few examples from various newspapers and if appropriate, read an advice column to children.

- Have children retell what happened to the kittens in the poem. Tell them that you have received a letter from the kittens asking for advice. Compose and read a letter such as the following:

Dear Children in Mrs. Thomas's Class,

We three kittens are always in trouble. Yesterday we lost our mittens again. Our mother was very unhappy. She said she doesn't want to buy more mittens. We also have trouble keeping our mittens clean. Yesterday, we ate some pie with our mittens on. They got berry stains all over them. What should we do?

Signed,

Three Sad Kittens

- Discuss what advice would help the kittens and then create a class-dictated letter to them.

- Invite children to decorate the letter with drawings of the kittens.

Take Another Look

If you had a kitten, what would you name it?

Write the name here.

MOSEY

PEPPER

chaff

Dear Little Kittens,

You better not lose your mittens again.

Put them in your pockets.

Why don't you come to our class to see where we put our things?

MAU

SPIKE

KITTY

PUFFY

tig

Words that Rhyme

- Reread the poem with children. Emphasize and point out rhyming words *kittens/mittens, dear/fear, cry/pie.* (If children notice, explain that the last word pair sounds alike but the words are spelled differently.) Have children say the words to hear the rhyming.

- Create a chart with three columns.

- Say and write the word *kittens* in the first and second columns and then have children suggest a word that rhymes. Record the word—*mittens.*

- Continue with other words. Remember that rhyming words can be nonsense words. Having children hear the rhyme is the key to the activity. If it is appropriate, explore how the end letters are the same but the beginning letters are different.

- Encourage children to read the chart throughout the week with different partners.

Take Another Look

Write words that rhyme with these.

Dog	Fat	Hen
hog	CAT	Pen
O	cAT	HOP
	(	
DOG	Sqr	

Words that Rhyme

kittens	kittens	mittens
jelly	jelly	belly
mother	mother	brother
jam	jam	ham
butter	butter	putter
silly	silly	billy
cat	cat	hat

Baby Animals

- Discuss the concept of animal babies. Show pictures and read books, such as *Baby Animals* by Angela Royston (Aladdin, 1991), *Animals at Home* by Jane Burton (Newington Press, 1991), or *Babies, Babies, Babies* by Tessa Dahl (Viking, 1991).

- List the names of baby animals on chart paper and then create sentences about each baby.

- Point to the words in the sentences as you read and reread them with children.

- Invite children to decorate the chart with drawings of baby and adult animals.

- Throughout the week, encourage children to read the chart with partners.

- Put a "Name this baby!" sign next to a different drawing each day and let children give the baby a name.

Take Another Look

Name this baby!

Write the names here.

Baby Animals

Kittens	are baby cats.
Puppies	are baby dogs.
Ducklings	are baby ducks.
Colts	are baby horses.

The Tortoise and the Hare

See another activity for this story on page 177.

Books to Read

Stevens, Janet. *The Tortoise and the Hare.* (Holiday House, 1984).

MacDonald, Suse. *The Tortoise and the Hare.* (Dial, 1990).

About the Story

Even very young listeners understand what is going on in this story before the characters themselves do. We love knowing more than the characters. We love being able to predict the ending of the story. That, perhaps, is the universal appeal of this story. We know the hare (rabbit) is silly to take a nap and rest during the race. We know the slow old turtle (tortoise) is going to somehow win. We are very satisfied that the rabbit loses because no matter how young we might be, we all know somebody who is puffed up and always thinks he or she is going to win. This story represents a type of justice to which all children can relate.

The story gives children opportunities to learn about how animals move, what turtles and rabbits are, and rules for doing things right, among other things.

Before introducing the story, explain the words *tortoise* and *hare,* using the more familiar animal names—*turtle* and *rabbit.*

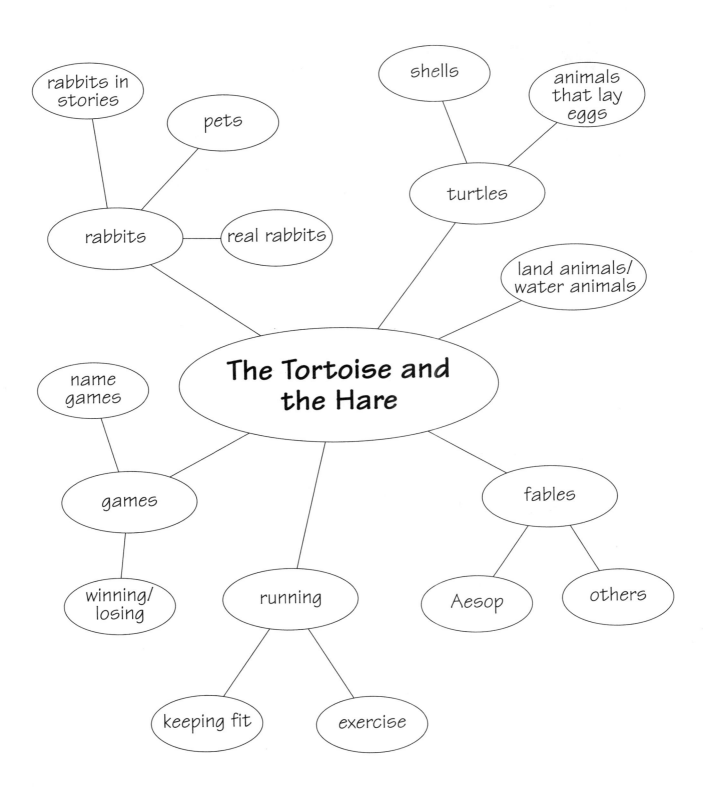

Rules for the Race

- Recall with children how the race began and ended and what the animals did during the race.

- Talk about the importance of setting rules when a game is played. Encourage children to talk about rules they know relating to basketball or baseball games.

- Help children understand that many rules are created for safety reasons.

- Decide on a time and a location for the class to participate in a running, skipping, or hopping race.

- Record the rules for the race as children suggest them.

- If you choose, remind children that as they were listening to the story for the first time, they were predicting or thinking about who would win the race. Invite them to predict who might win the class race.

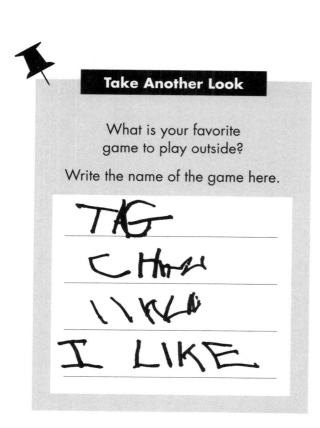

Take Another Look

What is your favorite game to play outside?

Write the name of the game here.

TAG

CHAS

11KLO

I LIKE

Rules for the Race

1. Everybody stand behind the line.

2. Wait until you hear "start."

3. Run as fast as you can.

4. Don't stop along the way.

Who do you think will win?

Jason

TOPIL

Billy   LILLY   SHANNA

PEDRO   CRISTAL

How Animals Move

- Recall with children how the animals in the story moved. Invite children to take turns pantomiming how animals move.

- Provide resource materials, photographs, and picture books so that children can look at and talk about various types of animals. Discuss where the animals live and how they behave.

- If possible, observe real animals in the class, or at a zoo, or an aquarium.

- Create a chart with three columns as shown in the sample. Invite children to name animals and tell in which column the names should be written on the chart.

- Reread the animal names as more are added.

- Invite children to illustrate the animals they named.

Take Another Look

Have you seen any animals today?

If you have, write the name of the animal here.

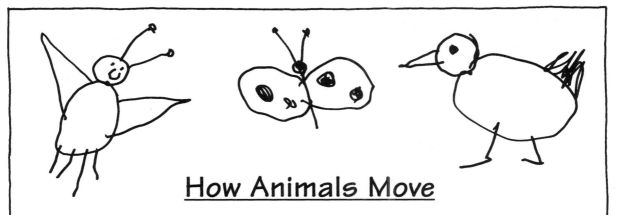

How Animals Move

On Land	In the Air	In Water
dogs	butterflies	whales
elephants	bugs	minnows
worms	robins	seals
cats	birds	otters
lions	bees	
lizards		

Our Turtle

- Tell children that a *tortoise* is a type of turtle that lives on land. It has stumpy legs and a high, round shell.

- Provide resource books, such as *Turtle Day* by Douglas Florian (Crowell, 1989) and *Box Turtle at Long Pond* by William T. George (Greenwillow, 1989), so that children can see what turtles look like and discover facts about them.

- If possible, observe a live turtle.

- Discuss things that are unique to turtles—hard shells, living both on land and in the water (amphibious), and egg-laying, for example, are facts that will make turtles memorable to children.

- Help children learn the poem "The Little Turtle" from *Collected Poems* by Vachel Lindsay (Macmillan, 1949).

- Invite children to dictate facts they have learned about turtles as you record them on a chart.

- Make a large outline of a turtle on the chart and have children provide a construction-paper, mosaiclike shell, with each child applying pieces of the mosaic. Add the head, feet, and tail.

Take Another Look

This big turtle needs a name.

What's a good one? Write it down.

GEN

BOBB

Our Turtle

Some turtles live on land.
Some turtles live in the water.
Turtles have a hard shell.
When they are scared,
they pull in their head.

A New Fable

- Explain that fables are stories that teach a lesson. What lesson did the story *The Tortoise and the Hare* teach? Children may need an explanation, such as *The rabbit learned that he shouldn't think he would automatically win the race because he was faster than the tortoise.* Aesop's lesson is: *Hard work and perseverance bring reward.*

- Read or tell additional fables children will understand, such as "The Stork and the Fox" by Aesop or the book *Fables* by Arnold Lobel (Harper, 1980).

- Note that fables often use animals to tell a story.

- Have children think about lessons they could tell in a fable of their own. Think about class rules that are created for safety, or topics such as kindness, happiness, cooperation, or sharing.

Take Another Look

Do you think the rabbit in the story learned a good lesson? Think about it and write your answer.

Yes, He Learned   **No, He Didn't**

A New Fable

Once there was a dog who

laughed when another dog

fell down.

Then he fell down.

Everybody laughed.

He didn't like it.

He cried.

Don't laugh when somebody

is in trouble.

Keeping Fit

- Discuss ways athletes or sports figures train and exercise so they are good at what they do. Make a list on the board of children's suggestions.

- Invite children to think about how they would train for a race and then recall the mistakes the rabbit made as he ran the race in the story.

- Have children compose a letter to the rabbit that includes tips about keeping fit for the next race.

- Record children's sentences on a piece of chart paper and then invite them to decorate the chart by drawing pictures of the rabbit.

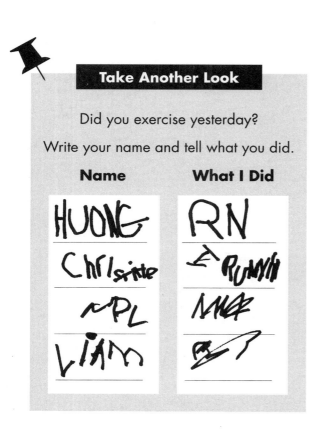

Take Another Look

Did you exercise yesterday?

Write your name and tell what you did.

Name	What I Did
HUONG	RN
Christine	I RUNN
MPL	NNE
LIAM	

Keeping Fit

Dear Rabbit,

Here's how to keep fit so you can win the race next time.

1. Eat vegetables.

2. Sleep at night.

3. Don't smoke.

4. Don't get tired.

5. Eat a good breakfast.

R Is for Rabbit

- Tell children that a *hare* is a type of rabbit that has long ears and long hind legs. In the United States, a jack rabbit is a hare, whereas a cottontail is a rabbit.

- Say the word *rabbit,* emphasizing the r sound at the beginning of the word. Write the word on a piece of chart paper and underline the letter *r.*

- Talk about each letter in the word *rabbit,* noting the double letters in the middle of the word.

- Sound out the word so that children can hear the sounds of each letter.

- Have children brainstorm other words that begin with the letter *r.* List them on the chart.

- Invite children to illustrate the words they suggested.

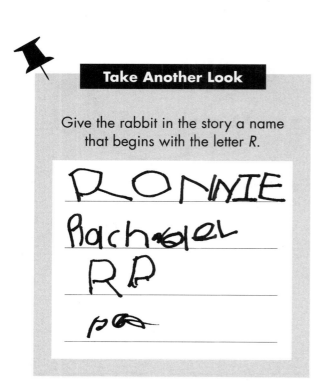

Take Another Look

Give the rabbit in the story a name that begins with the letter *R*.

R Is for Rabbit

Rr

rabbit

rainbow

radio

Robby

rug

See another activity for this story on page 177.

Books to Read

Butler, Stephen. *Henny Penny.* (Tambourine, 1991).

Zimmerman, H. Werner. *Henny Penny.* (Scholastic, 1989).

Kellogg, Steven. *Chicken Little.* (Morrow, 1985).

Palazzo, Tony. *Henny Penny and Chicken Little.* (Garden City, 1960).

About the Story

Henny Penny, Cocky Locky, Goosey Loosey, Ducky Lucky, and Turkey Lurkey are very, very silly birds. The silliest bird of all, Henny Penny, thinks the sky is falling when an acorn drops on her head. She gathers her friends so that they can go tell the king. Intent on their mission, they let their guard down as they meet Foxy Loxy. Depending on the version you read, the birds follow the fox into his cave, never to be seen again, or, they miraculously escape. Zimmerman's version is humorous and delightful. Kellogg's version is very funny and sophisticated. This story provides great opportunities for comparing different versions of the tale. Is the major character Henny Penny or is it Chicken Little?

The story provides an opportunity to think about birds, and to delight in the rhyming and the playfulness of language, among other things.

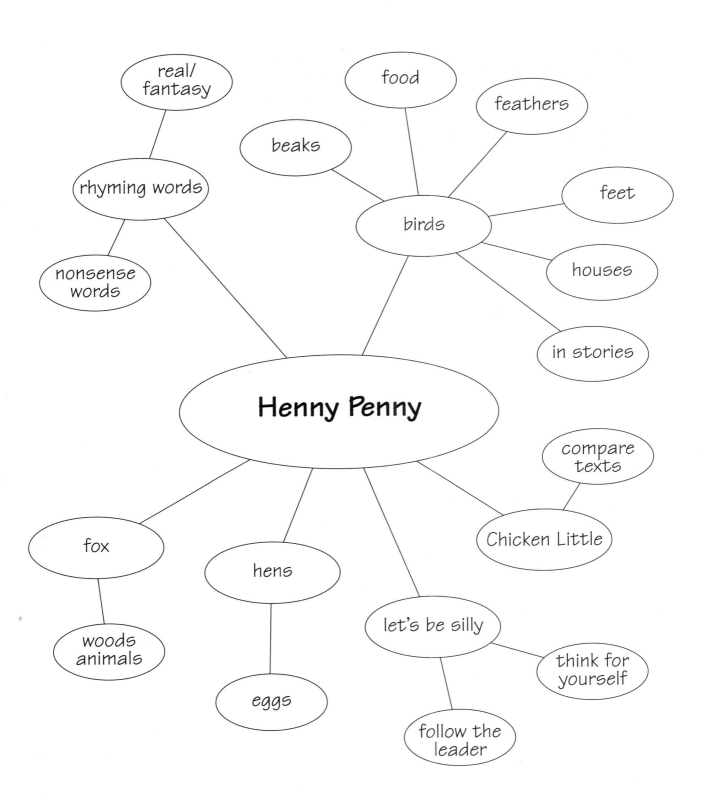

What Makes a Bird?

- Read books such as *Flap Your Wings and Try* by Nancy Tafuri (Greenwillow, 1989), *What Is a Bird?* by Ron Hirschi (Walker, 1987), *Feathers for Lunch* by Lois Ehlert (Harcourt, 1990), or *Pigeons* by Miriam Schlein (Crowell, 1989). Show children pictures of birds, and discuss birds' unique features.

- Go outside and observe birds. Talk about their movements—walking, hopping, bobbing, flying. Observe their shapes and colors. Talk about their legs and feet, their wings, beaks, and heads, and the shapes of their bodies.

- If possible, bring a pet bird into the classroom for observation. Look at bird nests and eggs.

- Invite children to recall their bird observations and then dictate bird facts as you record children's statements on a chart.

- Invite children to decorate the chart with drawings or construction-paper birds.

Take Another Look

Today at the art center,
draw your favorite bird.

What color is your bird?
What is the name of the bird?
Is it a big bird or a little bird?

What Makes a Bird?

Birds have feathers.

Birds have wings.

Birds can fly.

Birds have beaks.

Birds have two legs.

Birds lay eggs.

Who Lays Eggs?

- Show children a carton of eggs and have them share their experiences buying and eating eggs. Ask children to predict where eggs come from. Invite them to consider whether animals other than birds lay eggs.

- Create a chart listing the names of some animals that lay eggs and some that do not. Read the animal names with children and then invite them to record their predictions on the chart in the appropriate columns.

- After children's predictions are recorded, read books such as the following: *What's Hatching Out of That Egg?* by Patricia Lauber (Crown, 1979), *Chickens Aren't the Only Ones* by Ruth Heller (Grosset, 1981), and *Hatch, Egg, Hatch!* by Roddie Shen and Frances Cony (Little, Brown, 1991). The Heller book identifies all animals that lay eggs. If it is not available, be sure to include nature books about turtles and snakes.

- After reading and conversation, make a second chart duplicating the first one and then invite children to record their answers again.

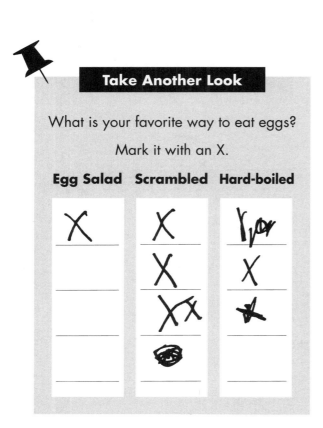

Take Another Look

What is your favorite way to eat eggs?

Mark it with an X.

Egg Salad	Scrambled	Hard-boiled

Guess! Who Lays Eggs?

You may be surprised!

	yes	no
birds	XXXXX	X
cats	X	XXXXX
snakes		XXXXX
dogs		XXXXXX
turtles	X	XXXXX

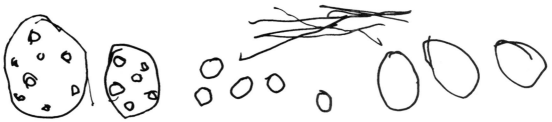

Silly Names

- After a reading of the story, list the names of the characters on the board, drawing attention to how the names rhyme. Explain that the ends of words that rhyme sound the same but the beginning of the words are different.

- Provide additional examples of names that rhyme, such as Piggy Wiggy, Randy Mandy, Judy Wudy, or Goatie Woatie. Then invite children to make up their own rhyming names. Ask them to keep their names a secret until it's their turn to contribute to the chart.

- If necessary, prompt children with the first names of the animals. Record the names as children suggest them. Invite children to say the names as they are recorded on the chart and enjoy the rhyming sounds of the names. Invite them to play with the language.

- Have children make drawings to accompany their rhyming names.

Take Another Look

Did you think of more silly names?

Write them here.

HENNY PENNY

DuckyLucky

FoxyLoxy

Silly Names

Goosy Loosy

Doggie Woggie

Catty Bratty

Mousie Wousie

Davie Wavie

Suzy Duzy

Percy Lercy

Fishy Wishy

A Treasure Hunt

- Recall that in the story, after an acorn dropped on Henny Penny's head, she went off to find the king. Explain that you, too, are going on a hunt to find the king. But before you get to the king, you must find objects to bring with you.

- Prepare a chart similar to the one shown that has simple treasure hunt directions relevant to your setting. Read each step with children. Make duplicate copies for each child or have children record on paper their own numbers and symbols for the objects to be gathered. (Read the chart more than once with children.)

- Provide small paper bags in which the objects can be collected.

- When children return to class, have construction paper available for them to use in creating their own king crowns.

Take Another Look

Make up your own treasure hunt for a friend.

Make it like this.

Find 1   STICK

Find 2   LEF

Find 3   FMZ

See if your friend can find everything.

Find the King: A Treasure Hunt

1. Go outside. Find one rock.

2. Find two sticks.

3. Go to the office. Find one paper clip.

4. Find one rubber band.

5. Go back to class. Make one crown.

   Put it on.

You have found the king!

Birds We See

- Have children name birds that they have seen and know live in the neighborhood.

- Create a chart listing the days of the week and the names of familiar birds, as well as birds that are not indigenous to your area. If possible, duplicate the chart for each child.

- Read the chart with children and explain that every day children should observe birds on their way to and from school. Or, plan to take children on a short walk each day to observe birds.

- Allow time each day to discuss which birds were seen and to record the observations on the class chart. It should become apparent which birds do and do not live in the area.

Take Another Look

Did you remember to look for birds today? Write your name under the YES or NO column.

Yes	No
CARLS LATTLA	Patrice RANDY

Did you record your observations?

Yes	No
d	

Birds We See

	M	T	W	T	F	S	S
crow	yes	yes	no	yes	yes		
robin	no	no	yes	no	no		
sparrow	yes	yes	yes	yes	yes		
magpie	no	no	no	no	no		
sea gull	no	no	no	no	no		
blue jay	no	no	yes	yes	no		

A New Story

- Talk with children about how they know the animals in the story are silly. What do the animals do that is very silly? Why do authors write stories that are silly? What do you do when you read or hear something silly?

- Encourage children to think of story lines that might be silly. What other things could animal characters do that would be as silly as Henny Penny thinking that an acorn falling on her head meant that the sky was falling?

- Have the class suggest characters to be featured in a new story and then create a class-dictated story following a pattern similar to that in *Henny Penny*.

- Write the characters' names on the chart and then record the story.

- Invite children to make their own drawings of the characters and to write a title of the story on their drawings. Display the drawings near the chart.

- Encourage children to create their own new stories at the writing table.

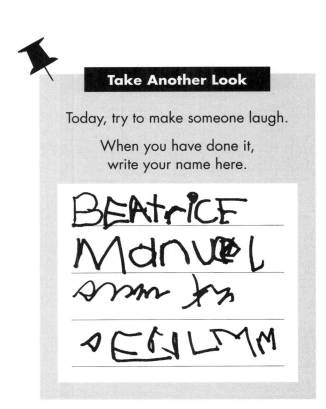

Take Another Look

Today, try to make someone laugh.

When you have done it,
write your name here.

BEATriCE

Manuel

A New Story

STARRING

Mousie Ousie

Beary Weary said, "My roof is coming down."

Puppy Wuppy said, "That's just the rain."

Mousie Ousie said, "That's just the rain."

Beary Weary said, "I'm going back to bed."

The End.

PUPPY WUPPY

BEARY WEARY

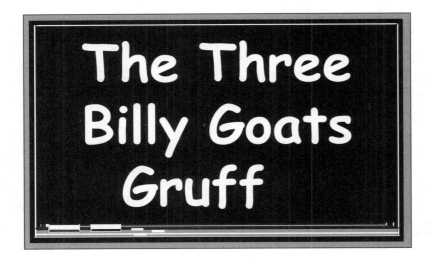
The Three Billy Goats Gruff

See another activity for this story on page 178.

Books to Read

Galdone, Paul. *The Three Billy Goats Gruff.* (Seabury, 1973).

Mayer, Marianna. *My First Book of Nursery Tales.* (Random House, 1983).

Haviland, Virginia. *The Fairy Tale Treasury.* (Coward, McCann & Geoghegan, 1972).

About the Story

Although many of us may not remember the first time we heard the story *The Three Billy Goats Gruff,* most of us recall that it was a story we heard often. And it was a story to which we reacted strongly. We were, perhaps, frightened by the troll. We could picture his saucer eyes, his terrible teeth, and his unkempt hair. We were, perhaps, enchanted by the bravado of the biggest billy goat. We responded, I imagine, with great anticipation, knowing deep in our hearts that if we were patient enough to wait for the biggest billy goat, the mean old troll would be served justice. Our enjoyment of the story was enhanced by the opportunities for sound devices as we trip-trapped over the bridge. Just you wait, you mean old troll! The biggest billy goat is coming!

This tale sets the stage for exploring all kinds of concepts, such as goats, water, trolls and elves, the number three, and sounds.

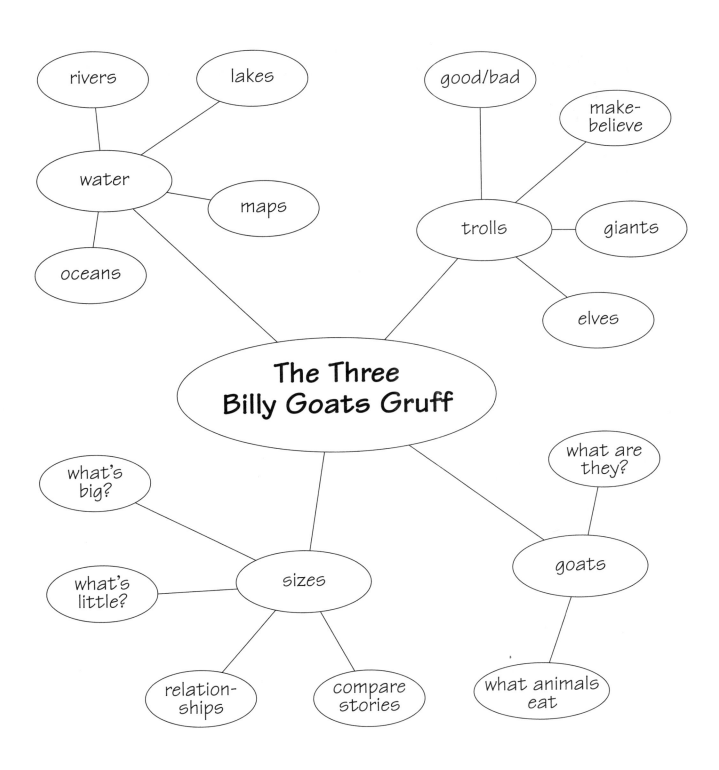

rivers

lakes

good/bad

make-believe

water

maps

trolls

giants

oceans

elves

The Three
Billy Goats Gruff

what are
they?

what's
big?

goats

what's
little?

sizes

relation-
ships

compare
stories

what animals
eat

What Do You Think Goats Eat?

- After reading the story, invite children to tell what they know about goats. Display a picture of real goats. Have children tell what other animals such as horses and cows eat and then invite them to think about what goats might eat.

- Prepare a chart similar to the one shown. Read the words with children. Then have them take turns predicting what they think goats might eat by making Xs in the YES or NO columns for each food listed.

- Count and total the votes.

- Use an encyclopedia or picture books about goats to confirm what goats do eat: corn, oats, cereal grains, hay, roots, silage, and commercial feed. Goats also like to eat leaves, grass, and various plants.

Take Another Look

If you had a goat, what would you name it?

Write the name here.

GOT

FLUFF

OK

VGINIAA

What do you think goats eat?
Will they eat . . .

		Yes!	No!
shoes		X	X X X
grass		X X X X	
dog food		X X	X X
flowers		X X X X	X
pizza			X X X
cereal		X X	X X

Let's find out what they really eat.

If I Were a Tiny Troll

- Use stuffed animals of varying sizes to discuss the concept of the words *little, small,* or *tiny,* and *big, bigger, biggest.* Have children name objects that are little, small, or tiny, such as insects, doll house furniture, miniature cars, and so on.

- Invite children to pantomime being tiny like trolls and being big like giants. How would they move? What kinds of steps would they take?

- Prepare the "If I Were a Tiny Troll" chart. Write the title of the chart and read it to children.

- Have children take turns adding to the chart their names, drawings of themselves as trolls, and labeled illustrations of people or things that would be bigger than they.

Take Another Look

Write the names of things that are bigger or smaller than you.

These are **Bigger.**   These are **Smaller.**

If I were a Tiny Troll this would be bigger

My Name	What's Bigger?
Troll Brian	My MOM
TROLL LUZ	MY DOG SPIKE
Troll Kaisha	My cat Melanie
TROLL GERMAINE	MY HOS

A Billy Goat Map

- Have children recall the story, thinking about its setting and events. You might want to have children close their eyes and visualize or imagine the setting. Talk about where the goats were living—on one side of the river—and the hill that the goats could see with the good grass on the other side. Talk about the bridge and where the troll must have lived. Help children visualize the green grass, the rushing river, and the bridge by asking questions, such as *How tall is the grass? Is it very green? Are there some wild flowers growing in the grass? Is the river deep or are there a lot of rocks and stones? Does the water feel very cold when you put your fingers in it?*

- Invite small groups of four or five children to make their own maps or drawings of the story. Encourage them to include the characters and to label their drawings.

- Have the groups compare their maps when they are completed.

Take Another Look

At the writing center, make a map showing where you live.

Show your house and your street.

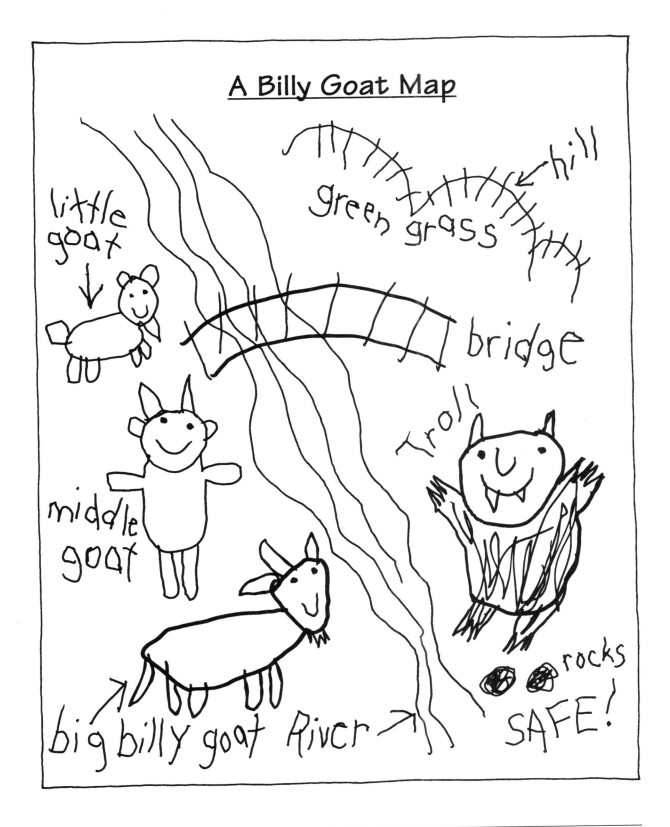

A Billy Goat Map

A Letter of Advice

- Invite children to talk about the differences between being happy and pleasant and being mean and grumpy. Children will be eager to share experiences they have had with other people's behavior. Encourage them to think about what makes people happy or grumpy. When do children feel unhappy or cranky? What makes them feel sad?

- Discuss the troll's behavior and have children speculate about why he seemed to be so unpleasant. Perhaps the troll didn't like himself very much.

- Invite children to contribute to a list of suggestions about how the troll could become more pleasant.

- Write children's sentences on a chart as they dictate them to you.

- Have children decorate the chart with their own drawings of the troll.

Take Another Look

Write your own letter to the troll. Give him some good advice.

Start your letter this way:

Dear Mr
TROLL

BE NICE

YU Or NOT!

Mrs. Classen's Advice Column

Dear Mr. Troll,

1. Don't be so mean.

2. Comb your hair!

3. Go to work!

4. Take a bath!

5. Leave the goats alone!

My Favorite Threes

- Recall with children the stories and rhymes you have read that have characters that come in threes—*The Three Bears, The Three Little Pigs,* "The Three Little Kittens," and *The Three Billy Goats Gruff.*

- Create a graph on a piece of chart paper similar to the example shown. Include the story or rhyme titles and simple drawings of the characters featured in each selection.

- Have children take turns making Xs in squares on the graph as they record their favorite story or characters.

- Total the numbers on the graph.

Take Another Look

At the writing center, write or draw your own story using three new characters.

What will happen in your story? Will there be dogs? bunnies? elephants?

My Favorite Threes

The Three Bears	X	X	X	X				4
The Three Little Pigs	X							1
The Three Kittens	X	X						2
The Three Billy Goats Gruff	X	X	X					3

Sounds I Hear

- Recall the sounds of the three billy goats tromping across the bridge. Have children imitate the goats walking.

- Read other books about sounds, such as Gene Baer's *Thump, Thump, Rat-a-Tat-Tat* (Harper, 1989), or Margaret Wise Brown's *The Seashore Noisy Book,* or Brown's *The Summer Noisy Book* (HarperTrophy, 1993), or Susan Schade and John Buller's *The Noisy Counting Book* (Random House, 1987).

- Invite children to close their eyes and listen to sounds they hear inside of and outside of the classroom.

- Take a walk outdoors to listen to noises.

- Write children's suggestions as they name loud and soft sounds on a chart.

- Encourage children to draw pictures of things that make sounds and attach their drawings as a border around the chart.

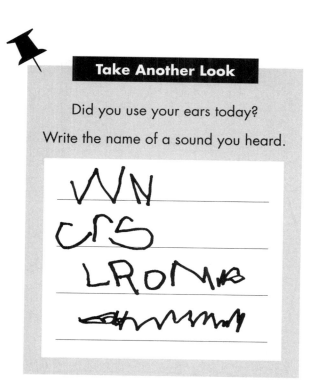

Take Another Look

Did you use your ears today?

Write the name of a sound you heard.

Loud	Soft
cars honking	music
doors slamming	my kitty
kids on the playground	the wind
the bell	chewing food

The Tale of Peter Rabbit

See another activity for this story on page 178.

Books to Read

Potter, Beatrix. *The Tale of Peter Rabbit.* (Puffin Books, 1991, by Frederick Warne. Based on the original published in 1902).

"The Tale of Peter Rabbit" from *A Treasury of Peter Rabbit and Other Stories* by Beatrix Potter. (Outlet Books, 1985).

The Big Peter Rabbit Book. (Warne, 1986).

Peter Rabbit's Colors. (Warne, 1988).

Peter Rabbit's Cookery Book. (Warne, 1986).

Garland, Sarah. *Peter Rabbit's Gardening Book.* (Warne, 1983).

About the Story

The suspense-filled story is a classic example of the price one pays for not doing what one's mother says, and the reward for good behavior.

Peter and his sisters are warned by their mother to stay out of Mr. MacGregor's garden. But Peter, enticed by the thought of succulent vegetables, disobeys his mother. He heads straight for the garden and feasts on radishes, carrots, and onions. He pays a price for his full tummy. Mr. MacGregor spies Peter and pursues him, creating a series of disasters for the trembling rabbit. After being soaked in a watering can, losing his jacket and shoes, Peter limps home. His mother puts him to bed and gives him a dose of chamomile tea, while Flopsy, Mopsy, and Cottontail, who are good little bunnies, have bread and milk and blackberries for supper.

Because Peter enjoyed them so much, let's explore luscious vegetables as we create print-rich activities.

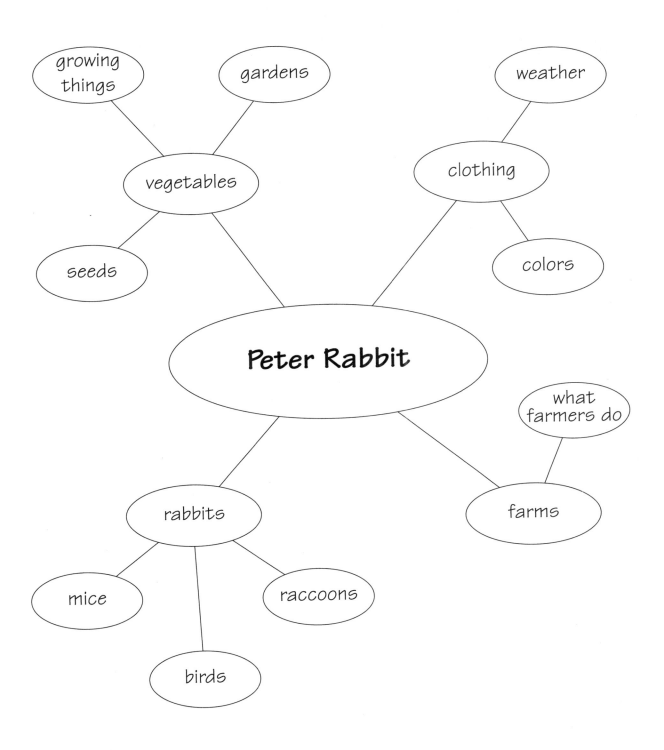

Vegetable Experience Charts

- While children recall the vegetables in Mr. MacGregor's garden, write the names of the vegetables on the board. Choose one vegetable to explore. Provide a sample, such as a carrot, a radish, or a zucchini.

- Pass the vegetable around so that each child can feel its texture and shape and look at it closely.

- Write the name of the vegetable at the top of a piece of chart paper. Talk about the letters in the word *(zucchini)* and the sounds the letters make. Note especially the letter *z* and the double *cc.* (Think how many vegetables have double letters!) Enjoy saying the word together.

- Have children take turns providing one word that describes a zucchini. Record the words on the chart.

- Give children green construction paper and invite them to make their own zucchinis. Ask each child where on the chart they would like to display their vegetables.

- Make individual zucchini-shaped books, with the descriptive words duplicated inside, for children to take home.

- Repeat this process for other vegetables. When completed, make comparisons between the charts, repeating the vegetable names and comparing the descriptive words.

Take Another Look

Write the name of your favorite vegetable here.

CrZ

LTTCE

salad

Carrots

orange   lumpy

long   dirty

bumpy   spotty

furry   fat

crunchy   hard

My Favorite Vegetable Graph

- Chat about Peter's favorite vegetables and then invite children to think about the vegetables you have explored together and to recall how they tasted. Did they taste strong? Were they crunchy? Did you like the colors of their skins?

- Choose three or four vegetables with which children are familiar.

- Create a graph on chart paper, writing the names of the vegetables in the first column and illustrating each with a construction-paper sample.

- Provide construction-paper scraps in the colors of the vegetables.

- Show children the graph and the size of the squares on the graph. Then invite them to choose their own favorite vegetables, make paper samples, and paste them on the graph in the appropriate places.

- Count the vegetables and record the totals on the chart.

- Encourage children to make their own charts for use in polling family and friends at home.

Take Another Look

Did you eat a vegetable today?

Write your name and the name of the vegetable here.

My Name	My Vegetable

My Favorite Vegetable

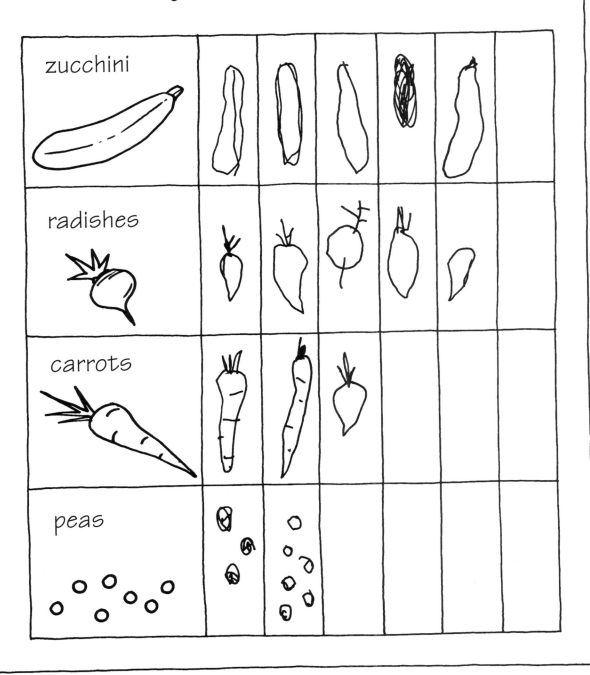

Vegetable Salad Recipe

- Before cooking together, write out a shopping list of ingredients for the salad. Because children will have had experiences tasting various vegetables, invite them to decide which ingredients to include in the salad.

- Write the salad recipe on chart paper, recording the steps in the process or directions for making the recipe.

- Illustrate the recipe as much as possible, including drawings or pictures of ingredients and utensils. Try to provide cooking experiences that can be carried out relatively independently by children, such as breaking or tearing foods into pieces, spreading soft ingredients, or cutting with plastic picnic-type knives.

- Read a recipe several times with children before asking them to follow the directions. If you are cooking as a class experience, read and point to each step before completing it.

- After a recipe is written on chart paper, invite children to decorate or border the writing as they work at the writing table.

- Duplicate recipes so that children can compile their own cookbooks or take the recipes home.

Take Another Look

At the writing table, make up a new vegetable recipe. How about Crunchy Carrot Cake? Red Radish Pudding?

Vegetable Salad

Tear up some lettuce.

Cut some carrots into pieces.

Make zucchini slices.

Make little pieces of tomato.

Add some cheese.

It's crunchy!

A Garden Mural

- Making a class mural can be a culminating activity after concepts have been fully explored. A garden mural stimulates thinking and conversation as children decide together how to approach the task. How do vegetables grow? Under the ground or above the ground? On vines or on plants? Are there roots? Do they have seeds?

- Prepare the background of the mural, showing sky and ground.

- Encourage discussion about what vegetables should be pictured on the mural. Make a list on the board and then invite groups of children to create different beds of vegetables, such as beans, radishes, or carrots. Discuss with each group what their particular vegetable looks like, and how and where it grows.

- Assist groups of children as they decide on the location of their vegetables in the garden.

- Create daily writing/thinking activities based on the mural similar to those shown.

Take Another Look

Would Peter Rabbit like this garden?

Mark your answer with an X.

Yes	No

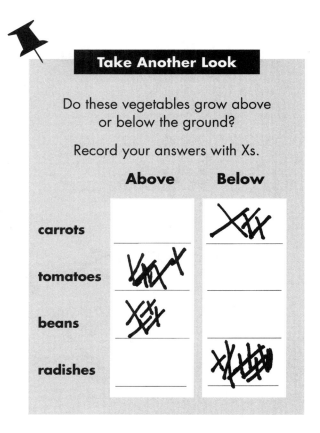

Take Another Look

Do these vegetables grow above or below the ground?

Record your answers with Xs.

	Above	Below
carrots		
tomatoes		
beans		
radishes		

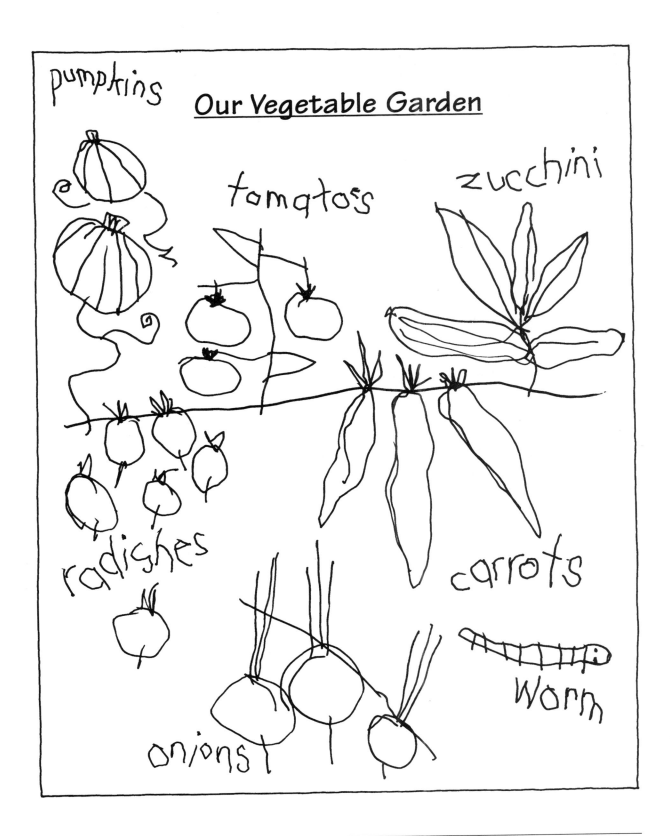

Write a Letter to Peter

- Read aloud a letter you yourself have received and encourage discussion about correspondence the children may have received.

- Talk about the greeting, the message, or saying what you want to say, and the closing of the letter.

- Invite the class to help you write a letter to Peter Rabbit. Recall with children Peter's mother's warning about Mr. MacGregor's garden and discuss what Peter did. Before you begin to record the actual letter, let children take turns telling what they think should be included in a letter to Peter.

- As you record, follow a letter format. Each time a sentence is added, reread the entire letter, beginning with the greeting to Peter, as you finger-point the words.

- Encourage all children to decorate the letter with their own construction-paper rabbits.

- Display the chart in the writing corner and invite children to write letters of their own to Peter, Mr. MacGregor, or Peter's sisters.

- Duplicate the letter and encourage children to read it to family members at home.

Take Another Look

Do you think Peter will ever go back into Mr. MacGregor's garden?

My Name	Yes	No
Margo	X	
Sylvan		X
Bobb	X	
LEE		X

Dear Peter,

You should have listened to your mother.

Don't ever go back to that garden.

Why can't you be good?

Your friends,

Mrs. Jack's Class

Create a New Story—What If?

- After children know the story well, write a "What if?" question on a piece of chart paper. Read the question to children at the beginning of the day and ask them to think about their answers throughout the day.

- Choose a time to chat together about children's answers to the question.

- Encourage children to write and illustrate their answers or to make up a new part to the story.

- Display their answers next to the question and invite your young authors to read what they've written to classmates.

Take Another Look

Be an author. Today, write a new story about Peter Rabbit and his family, Flopsy, Mopsy, and Cottontail.

What If?

What if Flopsy, Mopsy, and Cottontail had
gone to the garden with Peter?
What would have happened?

See more activities for this story on page 178.

Books to Read

Galdone, Paul. *The Little Red Hen.* (Seabury Press, 1973).

Hariton, Anca. *Egg Story.* (Dutton, 1992).

Martin, Antoinette Truglio. *Famous Seaweed Soup.* (Albert Whitman, 1993). A story parallel to *The Little Red Hen* in which a little girl makes seaweed soup all by herself.

McKissack, Patricia. *The Little Red Hen.* (Childrens Press, 1986).

Zemach, Margot. *The Little Red Hen.* (Farrar, Straus & Giroux, 1983).

About the Story

The Little Red Hen is the perfect story to read when dealing with the concept of helping. It is the perfect story because children have no difficulty with the justice that is dealt out by the hen. If you don't help make the bread, you won't get to eat it. It is plain and simple. The story's value lies not only in the just rewarding of behavior, but also in the teaching of sequence and story events. You can enhance children's understanding of the story when you include story props with the telling. Children need to see shafts and grains of wheat, flour, and breads. Unfamiliar vocabulary and concepts may require some expla-

nation, such as how wheat is cut with a scythe, or very sharp knife, and how, long ago, grain was ground or mashed into flour in a mill. (A pepper mill demonstrates the concept.) The repetitive structure of the hen's questions *"Who will help me . . . ?"* and the animals' responses, *"Not I," said the . . ."* invite children's active participation in the telling of the story.

The tale provides the perfect setting for exploring bread-making, planting and harvesting, farms, chickens and eggs, and, of course helping and cooperating, among other things.

A Helper Chart

- Discuss the concept of helping, inviting children to suggest ways in which they can help in the classroom.

- Prepare a chart, similar to the example shown, listing the days of the week and jobs. Read the chart with children, emphasizing the names of the days of the week.

- As you assign jobs for the week, invite children to write their own names in the appropriate spaces. Assure them that you will keep track of who has had a turn doing a specific job. Unlike the animals in the story, children are eager to help.

- Remind children to refer to the chart each day, to read the days of the week and one another's names.

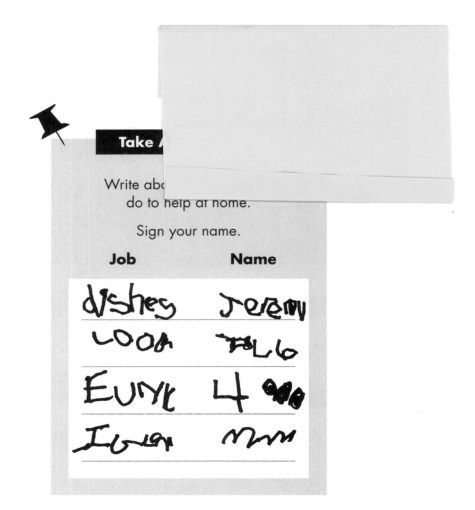

Take A

Write ab
do to help at home.

Sign your name.

Job   **Name**

dishes   Jeremy

LOOA   FOLG

EUIYL   4 one

IGIGI   mm

A Helper Chart

Who will?	
water plants	
Monday	KAISHA
Tuesday	Paulo
Wednesday	Vincent
Thursday	PATTY
Friday	Jerome
pass out milk	
Monday	Lynette
Tuesday	Harmon
Wednesday	Jita Lomas
Thursday	Justin
Friday	DARRYLL

We Made Rolls

- Provide the following ingredients for making a simplified version of cinnamon rolls: sugar, cinnamon, margarine, tube rolls.

- Invite children to mix the sugar and cinnamon (1/2 cup sugar and 1 tbsp. cinnamon) and separate the rolls.

- After melting margarine, have children dip the tops of the dough pieces in the margarine and then in the sugar and cinnamon mixture.

- Bake according to directions on the tube.

- After savoring the rolls, invite children to recall the steps in the process of making the rolls.

- Record the steps on chart paper as children dictate them.

- Duplicate the recipe for children to decorate and take home.

Take Another Look

What food do you think we should make or bake next?

Write your ideas here.

COOKY
Cakes
SOUP
Manny

We Made Rolls

1. Add 1 tbsp. cinnamon to 1/2 cup sugar.

2. Melt some butter.

3. Open a package of tube rolls.

4. Separate the rolls.

5. Dip the tops in butter.

6. Dip in the sugar.

7. Bake.

Vote for the Hen

- Recall with children the story ending and then have children talk about the hen's decision to not share the bread with the animals who didn't help. Do children think it was the right decision? Encourage children to think about how the other animals must have felt, and other choices the hen might have made.

- Invite children to talk about experiences they have had helping out or not helping out at home. Have they ever felt sorry that they didn't help when they could have or when someone did a job for them?

- Prepare a chart, similar to the example shown, and invite children to write their names and mark their votes answering the question.

- Have children predict whether there will be more *yes* or more *no* votes on the chart.

- Have children make drawings of the Little Red Hen on construction paper and attach them to the chart.

Take Another Look

How do you help at home?

Write down your favorite thing to do.

Vote for the Hen

Did the Little Red Hen do the right thing?

Name	Yes	No
Jason		
LUKE		
CINDY		
Latica		
Jerome		
RONDA		
RUPA		

A Feelings Chart

- Encourage children to imagine how the animals must have felt when they realized that the Little Red Hen was going to eat the bread all by herself.

- Talk about things that make children feel happy or sad. Share the thought that it is important that we know how we are feeling and how other people are feeling.

- Have children demonstrate how their faces look when they are happy and how they look when they are sad.

- Invite children to say whether they would feel happy or sad in response to imaginary situations, such as the following:

  You are all ready to go on a picnic at the park when it begins to rain hard.

  You are tucked in bed and your dad says you can read one more book before you go to sleep.

- Invite children to write their names and draw pictures of themselves looking happy and sad. Children can do this during free play or at their leisure.

Take Another Look

Think about whether you have made somebody happy today.

Write your name here when you think you have.

My Name	I'm Happy	I'm Sad
Justin		
Peter		
Samantha		
Raul		

Bread Spreads

- Read Nadine Bernard Westcott's *Peanut Butter and Jelly* (Dutton, 1987) and Russell Hoban's *Bread and Jam for Frances* (Harper, 1964).

- Provide bread, peanut butter, jelly, and another spread so that children can have a tasting party.

- As children eat, encourage them to think about and describe what they are tasting and how it feels.

- Pass out small brown, red, and yellow construction-paper squares that represent the various spreads.

- Prepare a chart similar to the example shown. Read the words at the bottom with children. Invite them to choose which spreads they like best and then attach representative squares in the appropriate columns.

- Total the squares to discover the all-time favorite.

Take Another Look

At the writing center, make up a silly sandwich. Write about or draw your sandwich. What's in it? How about a spaghetti fish sandwich? a hot dog and catnip sandwich?

Bread Spreads

5	3	3

Peanut Butter	Jelly	Butter

The Hen's Story

- After recalling the events in the story, have children imagine they are the Little Red Hen. Pantomime how she walks, flaps her wings, and puts on her apron.

- Invite children to suggest other chores the Little Red Hen might do around her house and pantomime how she does those activities.

- What do children think the hen would say if she were retelling her own story? Invite children to retell the story events as the Little Red Hen would. Is she disappointed with the dog, cat, and mouse? Is she feeling sad or angry?

- Write on the board the words *first, next* (or *then*), and *last*. Help children summarize the story into first, next, and last events from the hen's perspective.

- Record on chart paper a simplified first, next, and last story that children can read with you.

- Invite children to create their own versions of the story on paper.

Take Another Look

Who do you think will help the next time Little Red Hen makes bread?

Make an X under the animal's name.

Dog   Cat   Mouse

The Hen's Story

First, I 	asked my friends to help. 
Then, I 	did the work myself. 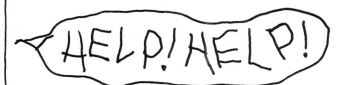
Last, I 	ate the bread myself.

See another activity for this story on page 178.

Books to Read

Brown, Marcia. *Stone Soup.* (Scribner, 1947).

Ross, Tony. *Stone Soup.* (Dial, 1987).

Stewig, John. *Stone Soup.* (Holiday, 1991).

Van Rynbach, Iris. *Stone Soup.* (Greenwillow, 1988).

About the Story

Does the stone really make the soup—that is, is the stone magic? This is the question and the mystery that most young children become involved with when they hear the story of the hungry soldiers who entice the villagers to share their precious food. Figuring out the function and purpose of the stone is, in itself, a sophisticated concept for story listeners. Because young children believe that magical things happen, they are often content to believe that the stone really did the trick. They like to believe that without it, the soup would not have been as tasty.

Understanding the soldiers' trickiness and craftiness as they convince the villagers to give up their food is a much more complex issue.

This twist on sharing can be perplexing for very young children. After reading this story to a kindergarten class and asking what the story was really about, a child responded, "It pays to be tricky." Remember to take into account the sophistication of the audience when discussing the moral or point of this story. The story is well loved by listeners who "get it," or figure it out. We love to see those selfish villagers tricked and outsmarted as they contribute to the soup.

One can't properly do this story without experiencing all kinds of soups. And don't forget how wonderful rocks are!

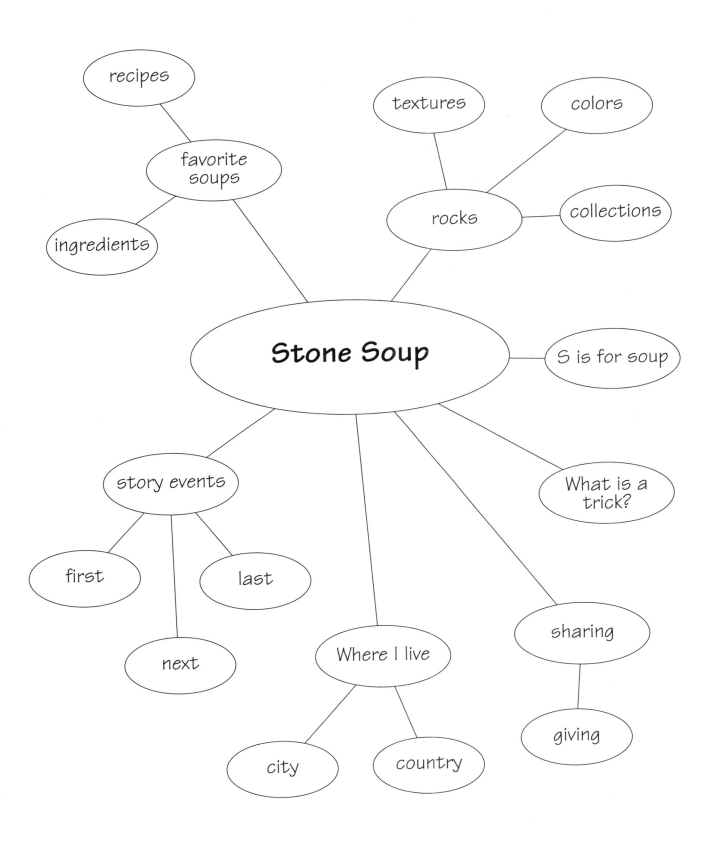

What Do You Share?

- After reading or talking about *Stone Soup* several times, read Pat Hutchins's *The Doorbell Rang* (Greenwillow, 1986) to stimulate a discussion about the concept of sharing. The Hutchins book gives young children a clear idea of the concept of sharing.

- Encourage children to talk about things that are appropriate for sharing and things that are not. Make lists, and then choose some items from each and transfer these to chart paper, making a chart similar to the example shown.

- When completed, read the words on the chart with children and then invite them to register their answers by making Xs in the appropriate columns.

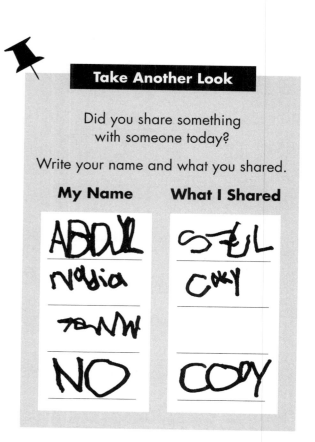

Take Another Look

Did you share something with someone today?

Write your name and what you shared.

My Name	What I Shared
ABDUL	STIL
Nadia	CaKY
TENW	
NO	CODY

What Do You Share?

	Yes	**No**
Do you share toys?	✗ ✗ ✗	✗
Do you share cookies?	✗ ✗ ✗ ✗	✗ ✗
Do you share vegetables?	✗ ✗	✗
Do you share a toothbrush?	✗	✗ ✗ ✗ ✗ ✗ ✗ ✗

My Rock

- Chat about the rock in the story and how it was used. What other things are rocks or stones used for?

- Talk about the properties of rocks—their shapes and textures, and where they are found.

- Go on a rock hunt outdoors, inviting children to choose a rock to bring back to class.

- Invite children to observe their rocks carefully, noting their smoothness or roughness, their shapes, and their colors.

- List describing words on the board as you chat.

- Prepare a chart identifying the colors of rocks. Have children write their own names on the chart and draw pictures of their rocks in the appropriate columns.

- Total the columns. Remind children that some people collect and study rocks.

Take Another Look

Do you have a collection?

Write your name and what you collect.

Name	My Collection
LUANE	pooch
Trini	NO
LUKE	LUN
sarah	off

My Rock

Name	black ■	brown ▨	gray ▨	white ☐
Corrine		⬤		
TYRONE				⬤
Latisha	⬤			
RAMON			⬤	
Eunice		⬤		
yunata			⬤	
Tony	⬤			
Total	2	2	2	1

A Letter to the Village

- Write a short letter on the board or read aloud a letter you have received to remind children what is included in a letter.

- Invite children to pretend that they are the soldiers in the story, and they want to write a thank-you note to the villagers.

- Have children talk about what they want to say in a letter to the villagers, and then record their dictations as they collaboratively make suggestions.

- Invite them to decorate the letter with illustrations of the soldiers or pictures of themselves.

Take Another Look

What do you think was the name of the village that the soldiers visited? Give the village a name.

Write the name here.

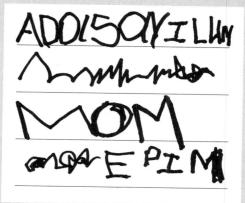

Dear Friends,

The soup you made was very good.

In fact, it was delicious.

That rock must be special. Hope we can come visit again.

The Soldiers

YUM!

Make Silly Soup

- List on the board the ingredients that went into the soup in the story: carrots, potatoes, meat bones, and so on.

- Have children talk about soups they have eaten and list ingredients they think are in those soups.

- Then tell children that they are to make up a list of ingredients that would go into a very silly soup.

- On chart paper, list the numbers 1 through 10. Begin the ingredients with one stone or rock. Then have children suggest other ingredients that would make good, silly soup.

- At a later time, have volunteers take turns illustrating the list with the appropriate number of ingredients.

- After reading the list several times, hand out pieces of paper and ask the children to write how the soup tastes. Remember, it is not important that children write conventionally. Encourage them to write any way they can. Usually, they can read their own writing to you.

Take Another Look

If you made your own silly soup, what would you put in it?

CNDY

SGTI

Silly Soup

1 rock

2 potatoes

3 frogs

4 candy bars

5 jelly beans

6 peanut butter

7 bubble gum balls

8 apples

9 macaroni

10 cakes

S Is for Soup

- Say the word *soup*, emphasizing the s sound at the beginning of the word. Pretend to *sip* and *sniff* some *steaming soup*.

- Invite children to suggest other words that begin with the letter *s*. Write the words on chart paper as they are suggested.

- Underline the initial letter as you say each word.

- Have children take turns pointing to and saying individual words.

- You may choose to make simple illustrations for each word to help children read the words independently if you display the chart in the room. Encourage children to make additions to the chart as they discover words that begin with *s*.

Take Another Look

Write your own word that begins with the letter *S* here.

(This activity can change daily to cover action words or proper names.)

S is for

S Is for **S**oup

soap

sun

swim

snow

spaghetti

socks

seal

snowsuit

soup

Sondra

S is for **S**illy

Our Favorite Soups

- Encourage conversation about soup. Invite children to describe when they like to eat soup and what their favorite soups taste like.

- Record the names of some soups on a bar graph similar to the example shown. Record only an appropriate number of choices.

- After reading the names of the soups, invite children to color in squares on the graph, determining which soup is most popular.

- Total the results and celebrate the winning soup by sampling it at a soup lunch or at snack time.

Take Another Look

Write the name of your favorite soup here.

Our Favorite Soup

The Winner!

4	1	2	5	1
			▓	
▓			▓	
▓		▓	▓	
▓	▓	▓	▓	▓
chicken noodle	bean	tomato	chili	vegetable

Five Little Monkeys

See another activity for this story on page 178.

Five little monkeys jumping on the bed,
One fell off and bumped his head.
Called for the doctor and the doctor said,
"No more jumping on the bed!"

Four little monkeys jumping on the bed,
One fell off and bumped his head.
Called for the doctor and the doctor said,
"No more jumping on the bed!"

Three little monkeys jumping on the bed,
One fell off and bumped his head.

Called for the doctor and the doctor said,
"No more jumping on the bed!"

Two little monkeys jumping on the bed,
One fell off and bumped his head.
Called for the doctor and the doctor said,
"No more jumping on the bed!"

One little monkey jumping on the bed,
He fell off and bumped his head.
Called for the doctor and the doctor said,
"No more monkeys jumping on the bed!"

Books to Read

Christelow, Eileen. *Five Little Monkeys Jumping on the Bed.* (Clarion Books, 1989).

_____. *Five Little Monkeys Sitting in a Tree.* (Clarion Books, 1991).

About the Rhyme

This fun-filled nursery rhyme can jump-start additional rhyming/counting activities, such as fingerplays, and innovating on the text. The topic of monkeys delights children as they discover monkeys' antics and mischief-making.

Children will enjoy comparing books about real-life monkeys with those about make-believe monkeys, such as Curious George.

Ready for rhyming activities and monkey fun?

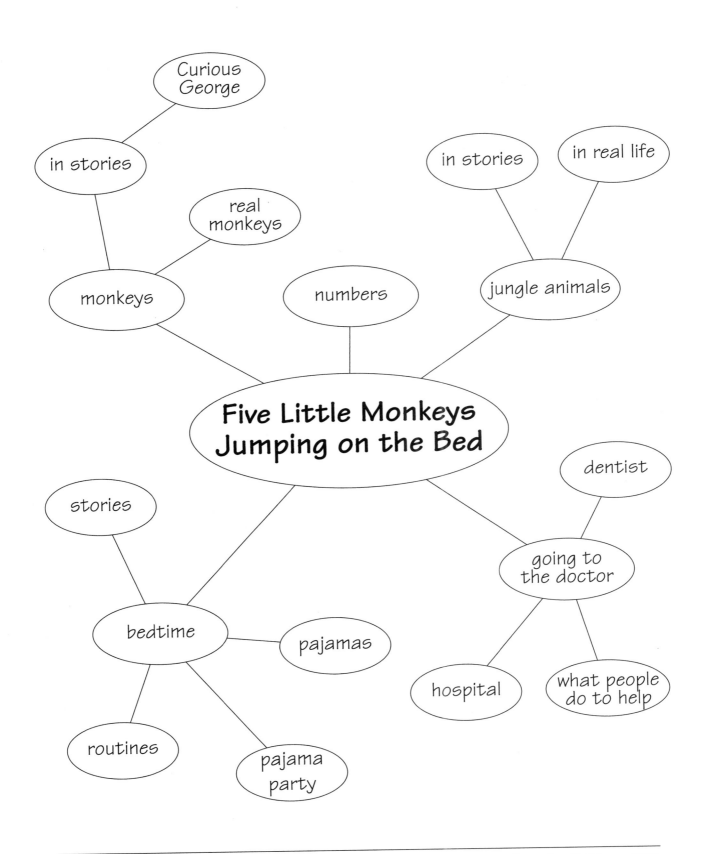

Our Monkey Rhyme

- After children have learned the rhyme and repeated it many times, write the rhyme on chart paper so that children can read along as you point to the words.

- Draw children's attention to rhyming words, such as *bed* and *head.*

- Have children brainstorm other places from which monkeys could jump and think of resulting actions, such as *One little monkey swinging from a tree, she fell off and broke her knee,* or *Four little monkeys jumping on the sink, one fell off and she turned pink.*

- Record children's sentences as they create them, offering assistance as needed. Encourage all children to decide whether the words suggested in each phrase are rhyming words.

Take Another Look

Write a word that rhymes with the words you see.

Pig	Bed
Big	red
FHI	bed
ZZZ	Sed
pig	

Our Monkey Rhyme

5 Five little monkeys jumping from a **tree,**

One fell off and hurt his **knee.**

4 Four little monkeys jumping on the **door,**

One fell off and landed on the **floor.**

3 Three little monkeys jumping on a **chair,**

One fell off and hurt his **hair.**

2 Two little monkeys jumping in the **snow,**

One fell down and broke his **elbow.**

1 One little monkey jumping in the **bus,**

He fell down and made a **fuss.**

A Five Rhyme

- Write the familiar Mother Goose rhyme on chart paper as shown in the sample, listing the number words vertically. Leave room for fish to be drawn next to the number words.

- Say the rhyme several times with children, counting from 1 to 5 on fingers.

- Have children guide you and collaborate as you decide how many fish to draw next to each number word, or invite volunteers to draw the fish.

- Invite each child to take a turn writing the numeral 5 and then drawing five objects on the borders of the chart, or provide pieces of paper on which children can draw the objects and write the numeral to be attached to the chart as a decorative border.

Take Another Look

Look around the room for the number 5.

Do you see it anywhere?
Write the number here.

A Five Rhyme

One

Two

Three

Four

Five

I caught a fish alive.

Why did you let him go?

Because he bit my finger so!

My Bedtime

- Invite children to talk about their bedtime routines, such as clothing they take off and put on, hygiene procedures, snacks, and stuffed toys they might take to bed with them. Does someone read a book to them before they go to sleep?

- Children will enjoy your sharing some of your going-to-bed routines with them. Do you put your slippers under the bed? Do you fluff up your pillow or have a glass of milk? Do you give your dog a snack or put out the cat?

- Choose four or five common bedtime activities and write them on a chart similar to the one shown.

- Invite children to record whether or not each activity listed is a part of their bedtime routines by writing an X or their names in the YES or NO columns.

Take Another Look

Do you have a favorite toy you take to bed with you?

Write the name of your toy here.

teddy
Brni

My Bedtime

	YES	NO
Put on pajamas	X X X X X X	
Wash my face	X X X X	X X
Brush my teeth	X X X X X X X X X	X
Read a book	X X X	X X X X X
Turn out the light	X X X X X X X X X	

How Many Bananas?

- Create a chart graph with the numbers 1 through 5 written in random order at the bottom of the graph.

- Provide yellow construction paper so that each child can make a banana to contribute to the chart.

- Identify the numbers on the chart with children and then invite them to take turns attaching their bananas to the graph, placing them in rows so that the number of bananas corresponds to the numerals.

- Encourage children to negotiate with and help one another as they decide whether the appropriate number of bananas appears in each column.

Take Another Look

Do you like bananas?

Write your name under Yes or No.

Yes   **No**

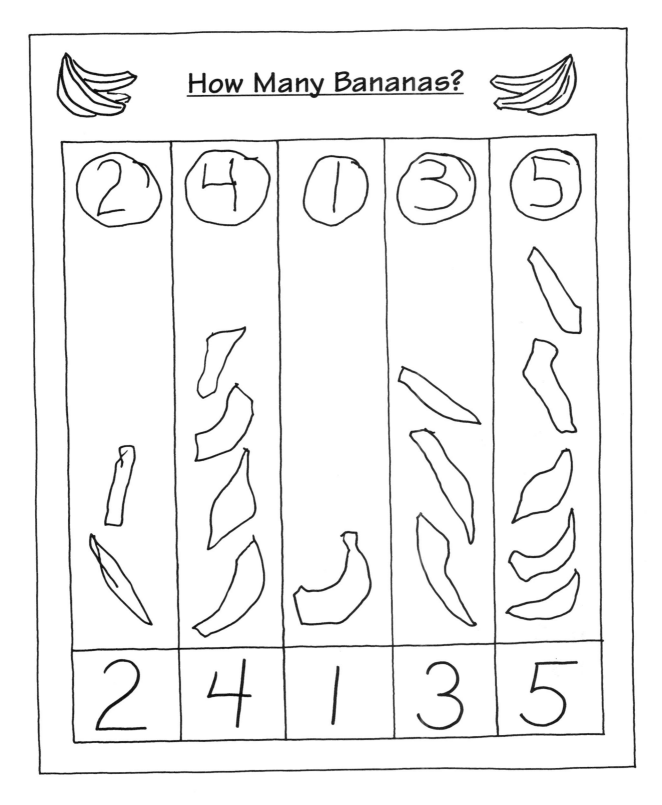

How Many Bananas?

Head, Shoulders, Knees, and Toes

- Sing the song "Head, Shoulders, Knees, and Toes" with children.

- Identify body parts and talk about how we move various parts of our bodies.

- Draw a large, simple outline of a human on chart paper.

- Write the names of various body parts, such as *head, elbow, fingers,* and *chest* on word cards.

- Distribute the word cards and invite volunteers to help figure out and identify each word.

- Have children take turns attaching the words to the appropriate locations on the figure.

- Repeat this activity several times and encourage children to do it independently throughout the week.

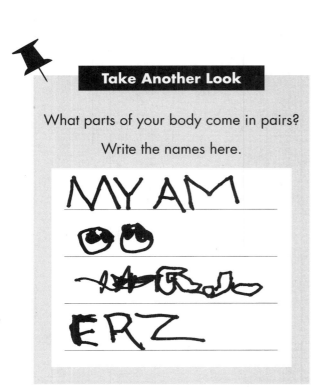

Take Another Look

What parts of your body come in pairs?

Write the names here.

MY AM

ERZ

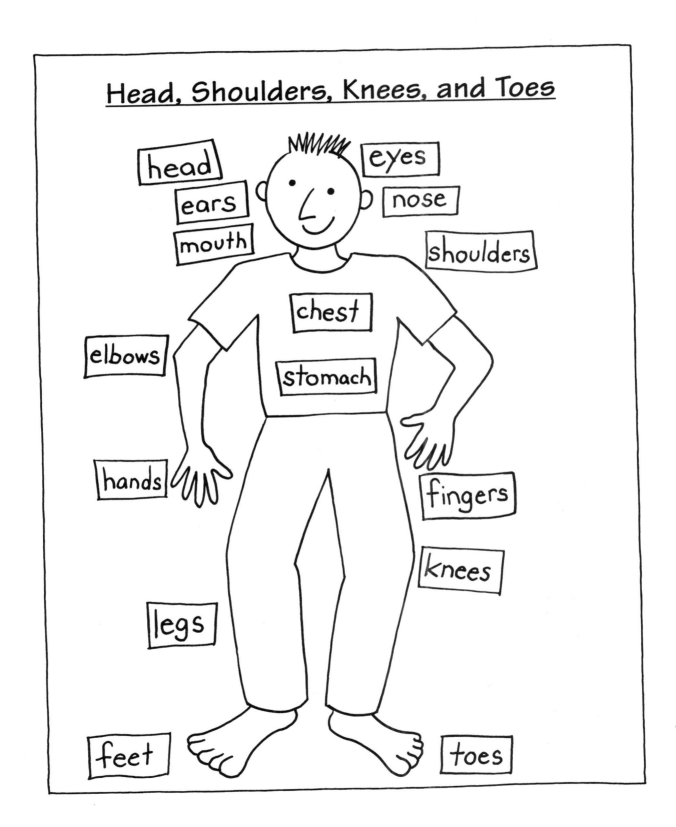

Head, Shoulders, Knees, and Toes

head

eyes

ears

nose

mouth

shoulders

chest

elbows

stomach

hands

fingers

knees

legs

feet

toes

M Is for Monkey

- Write the first line of the rhyme on the chalkboard or refer to the rhyme written on a chart.

- Underline the word monkeys in the first line and then have children locate and underline the word in the other sentences.

- Draw attention to the letter *m*. Have children say the word monkeys with you, emphasizing the m sound.

- Write a capital and a lower-case m on a piece of chart paper. Label the chart "M Is for Monkey."

- Invite children to suggest other words that begin with the letter *m* and write them on the chart.

- Read the words several times with children and then ask them each to write a capital and a lower-case *Mm* on the chart.

- Illustrate the *m* words with simple line drawings if you wish.

Take Another Look

Give this monkey a name that begins with the letter M.

M Is for Monkey

Mm

Michael

Mora

money

mittens

Monday

milk

mud

See another activity for this story on page 178.

Humpty Dumpty sat on a wall,
Humpty Dumpty had a great fall.
All the king's horses and all the king's men,
Couldn't put Humpty together again.

Books to Read

Hayes, Sarah. *Bad Egg: The True Story of Humpty Dumpty.* (Little, Brown, 1987).

Mother Goose Books

Invite children to compare illustrations in various volumes of Mother Goose. They will see Humpty Dumpty depicted in many ways. In *Ring O'Roses: A Nursery Rhyme Picture Book* (originally published in 1922), the illustrator, L. Leslie Brooke, draws the story of Humpty Dumpty on four pages. *Michael Foreman's Mother Goose* includes a spectacular painting of a fallen Humpty Dumpty, and James Marshall provides an unusually naughty Humpty in his characteristically humorous style. Children will be able to visualize the silliness of the rhyme and the character as they compare interpretations.

Brooke, L. Leslie. *Ring O'Roses: A Nursery Rhyme Picture Book.* (Clarion Books, 1992).

Foreman, Michael. *Michael Foreman's Mother Goose.* (Harcourt, 1991).

Marshall, James. *James Marshall's Mother Goose.* (Farrar, Straus & Giroux, 1979).

About the Rhyme

The rhythm and cadence of this rhyme have delighted children for generations. Two-year-olds clap and chant the rhyme, while preschoolers and kindergartners enjoy speculating about who and what Humpty really is. Is he *really* an egg? Is he good or bad? What kind of clothes did he wear? The spirit and mystery of the rhyme invite fun-filled predictions and investigations. Humpty Dumpty provides a forum for investigating shapes, safety, and rhyme.

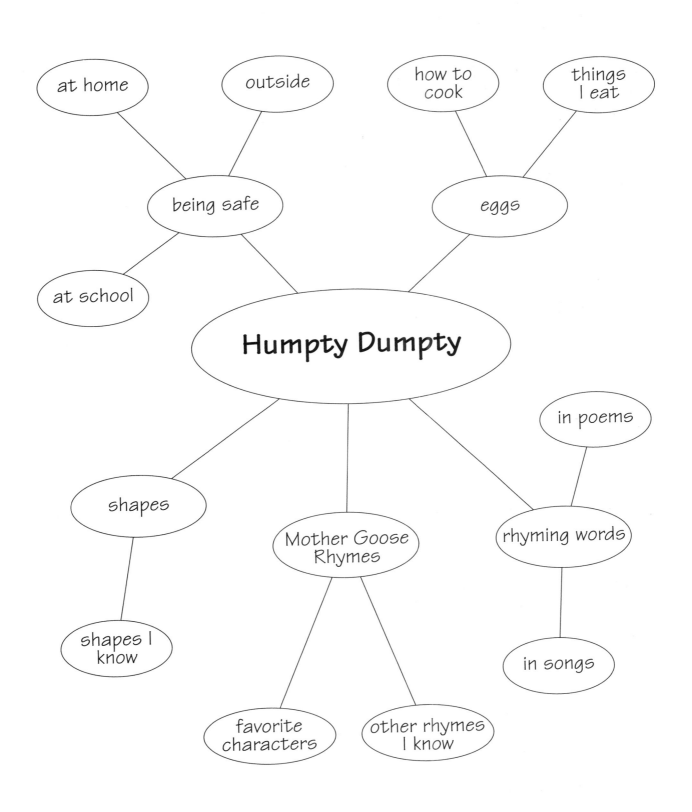

Fix Up Humpty

- After children are familiar with the rhyme, chat about Humpty Dumpty's accident. How do children think the accident happened? Why did he fall off of the wall? Did he try to stand up? Was he laughing too hard? Was he being silly? Then have children share experiences they have had with breaking objects or falling down.

- Talk about how things are repaired when they are broken. Have children used bandages? glue? tape? Invite children to suggest how Humpty could best be repaired after his fall.

- Choose three or four suggestions children make for repairing Humpty Dumpty and create a chart similar to the example shown. Have children think about the best way to repair Humpty and then invite them to write their names and identify the materials they would use to fix up Humpty Dumpty.

- Provide bandages, tape, and staples. Invite children to make their own Humpty Dumptys and fix them up.

Take Another Look

Fix up Humpty Dumpty!

Choose one place to put a bandage on Humpty.

Use a crayon to draw the bandage.

Fix Up Humpty

Put Humpty Dumpty together again with...

glue	RASHA	Jamie	Lohren	
staples	Sarah	VENUS		
tape	ERIC	KISHA		
pudding	Ramon	HANNA	Billy A.	
	Aaron			

More Humpty Dumpty Rhymes

- Write the rhyme on chart paper. Have children identify the rhyming words *hill/spill* and *men/again*.

- Invite children to brainstorm other places where Humpty could sit and have a resulting action, using rhyming words. Invite children to come up with nonsense phrases. The rhymes don't have to make sense.

- Write children's new rhyming couplets on the chart.

- If necessary, you provide the first lines and have volunteers provide the next lines. Consider using the following:

Humpty Dumpty sat on a chair . . .
Humpty Dumpty sat on a rug . . .
Humpty Dumpty sat on the floor . . .
Humpty Dumpty sat on a hat . . .
Humpty Dumpty sat on a car . . .

Take Another Look

Think of the king in the
Humpty Dumpty rhyme.
What do you think the king's name is?
Give the king a good name.

Write the name here.

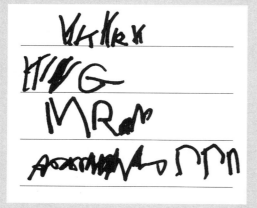

More Humpty Dumpty Rhymes

Humpty Dumpty sat on a hill,

Humpty Dumpty had a great spill,

All the King's horses and

All the King's men,

Couldn't put Humpty together again.

Humpty Dumpty sat on a cat.

Humpty Dumpty went splat.

Humpty Dumpty sat on a cow.

Humpty Dumpty cried "wow!"

My Shape

- Remind children that Humpty Dumpty was shaped like an egg. Bring in an egg so that children can see its distinctive shape.

- Initiate a discussion about shapes, inviting children to name and identify shapes they know.

- Prepare a chart similar to the example shown. Make sample shapes in the first column and write the names of the shapes. Make each shape a different color.

- Distribute pre-cut construction-paper shapes to children and have them find the appropriate columns in which to attach their shapes, or invite children to draw outlines of their favorite shapes in the appropriate columns.

- If children are choosing their favorite shapes, tally up the totals to discover the all-time favorite.

Take Another Look

Today, cut out a little square and paste it here.

Use paper from the art corner.

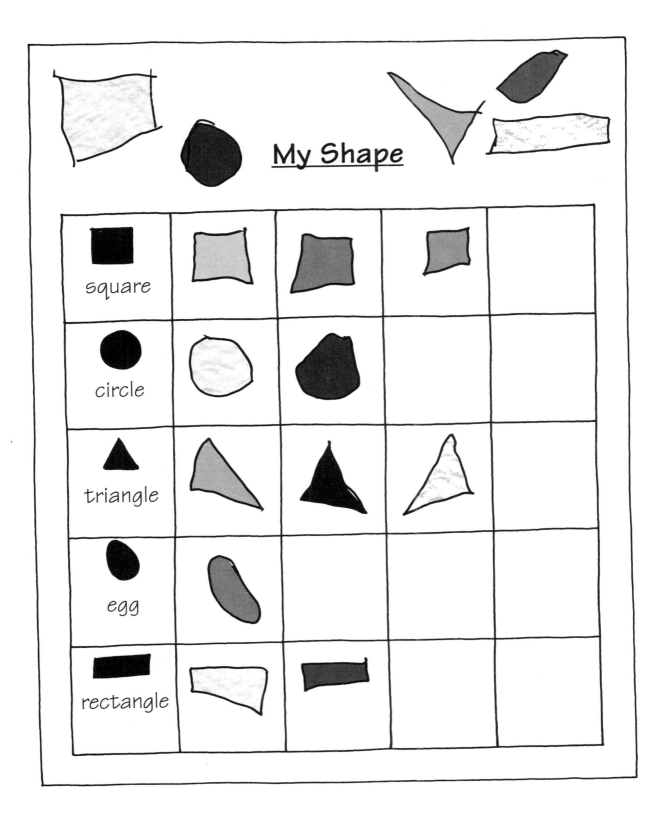

My Shape

	square	circle	triangle	egg	rectangle

Our Favorite Mother Goose Rhyme

- Invite children to chant Mother Goose rhymes they know and enjoy.

- Choose four rhymes and invite groups of children to illustrate each rhyme.

- Display the illustrations on a chart or bulletin board and label them for children. Read the words with children.

- Invite children to vote for their favorite rhymes by making a check mark or an X, or by writing their names, in the appropriate spaces.

- Tally up the votes as children count the marks with you.

- Invite children to explain why the rhymes are their favorites.

Take Another Look

Who is your favorite nursery rhyme character?

Make an X by his or her name.

Jack and Jill

Little Boy Blue

Humpty Dumpty

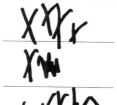

Our Favorite Mother Goose Rhyme

Jack and Jill went up the hill . . .	✓ ✓ ✓
	✓ ✓ ✓ 6
Little Boy Blue come blow your horn . . .	✓ 1
Humpty Dumpty sat on a wall . . .	✓ ✓ ✓ ✓
	✓ ✓ ✓ 7
Mary, Mary quite contrary . . .	✓
	1

A Letter to Humpty Dumpty

- Involve children in a discussion about being safe. Help children describe situations and places in which they can be alert to safety. How do they stay safe and accident-free at home, outside, or in school?

- Make lists of suggestions on the chalkboard or on chart paper.

- Then invite children to compose a letter to Humpty Dumpty, giving him good safety tips.

- Record the tips on chart paper as children suggest them.

- Invite children to sign the letter by drawing pictures of themselves or by writing their names.

Take Another Look

Did you think about safety rules on your way to school today?

Yes	Not Really
MORA	Liam
Mroor	Cherry
Lisa	
BILLY	

Dear Humpty Dumpty,

Here's how to stay safe.

1. Listen to your parents.

2. Look before you cross the street.

3. Don't run in school.

4. Don't ride your bike into someone.

From your friends in Mrs. Sanchez's class

PETER
PAULA
LADONNA
CELIA
JEREMY

Make Egg Boats

- Prepare hard-boiled eggs and construction-paper sails in advance.

- Demonstrate each step in the process of making egg boats.

- After you have demonstrated the process, have children recall the steps while you record their dictations on chart paper.

- Point to and read all of the directions before inviting children to make their own egg boats.

- Display the recipe chart and invite children to use it as a model for writing their own recipes that they can take home with them.

Make Egg Boats

1. Cook some eggs in the shell. They have to be hard.

2. When they cool, crack and peel them.

3. Slice the eggs in half.

4. Make paper sails.

5. Put toothpicks on them.

6. Stick them into the eggs.

Take Another Look

This is how much I liked eating egg boats yesterday.

Make an X under the words.

Yummy	**Not so Yummy**

Patterns and Charts for Each Story

Directions

The patterns and charts on the following pages can be used in conjunction with each of the stories in *Charts for Children*.

Goldilocks and the Three Bears

Pattern: cereal box .... page 179

Invite children to decorate a pretend cereal box, including the name of their favorite cereal or of an imaginary cereal they create. Write the cereal names for children as they dictate to you.

The Three Little Pigs

Pattern: house .... page 180

Invite children to color and decorate their own house. Talk about the shapes that make up the house. Identify the door, window, roof, and chimney. Compare the house to that of the Three Little Pigs.

The Gingerbread Man

Pattern: gingerbread person .... page 181

Make copies of the pattern on brown or tan construction paper. Provide decorative materials, such as glitter, buttons, candies, or bright papers so children can glue them to the cookie.

The Three Little Kittens

Pattern: mittens .... page 182

Have children cut out pairs of mittens and decorate them with designs that will make an identifiable pair. Use the mittens to complete the mitten chart in Activity 1 on page 54.

The Three Little Kittens

Chart: Words that Rhyme .... page 183

Reproduce the chart so that children can share it with their families at home. Read the rhyming words several times with children, encouraging them to finger-point the words as you read. Use this with Activity 5 on page 62.

The Tortoise and the Hare

Pattern: turtle .... page 184

Children can color the turtle or they can cover the turtle with torn bits of green construction paper, gluing them on to make a collage-type shell, such as that shown in Activity 3 on page 72.

Henny Penny

Pattern: bird .... page 185

Identify the features on the bird pattern, such as the tail, wings, beak, and legs. Supply feathers for gluing onto the bird, or provide markers or crayons for decorating.

The Three Billy Goats Gruff

Chart: Counting .... page 186

Identify the numerals on the left-hand side of the page. Count the corresponding numbers of goats. Then invite children to practice writing the numerals 1 to 3 in the squares on the right side of the page.

The Tale of Peter Rabbit

Pattern: vegetable squares .... page 187

Invite children to color each vegetable after identifying what colors the vegetable should be. Have children cut out the squares, following the cutting lines. These squares can be used to complete the graph in Activity 2 on page 112.

The Little Red Hen

Pattern: bread slice .... page 188

Invite children to cut out the slice of bread, following the cutting line. Provide colored construction paper ingredients, such as brown bologna, yellow cheese, green lettuce, and red tomatoes, helping children create their own paper sandwich.

The Little Red Hen

Chart: We Made Rolls recipe ..... page 189

Make copies of the recipe so children can share it with family members and bake at home. Before sending it home, have children decorate the page with pictures of ingredients or baking tasks.

Stone Soup

Pattern: soup bowl .... page 190

Have children cut out the soup bowl, following the cutting lines. Provide colored construction paper scraps, encouraging children to cut or tear paper ingredients to glue onto their bowl.

Five Little Monkeys

Chart: My Bedtime .... page 191

After talking about healthy bedtime routines when completing the chart in Activity 3 on page 156, copy and distribute this chart so that children can record their own activities at home.

Humpty Dumpty

Pattern: egg .... page 192

Encourage children to color and decorate a Humpty Dumpty pattern using various collage materials, markers, and crayons. Encourage children to make Humpty's face, showing how the egg feels.

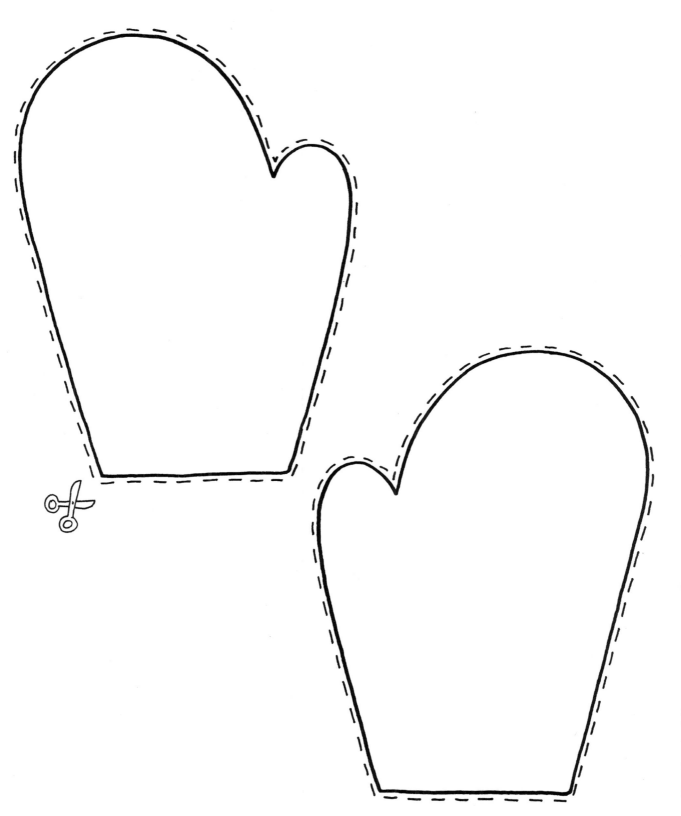

Name _____

Words that Rhyme

kittens	kittens	mittens
jelly	jelly	belly
mother	mother	brother
jam	jam	ham
butter	butter	putter
silly	silly	billy
cat	cat	hat

Name _____

1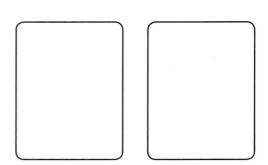

2 

3

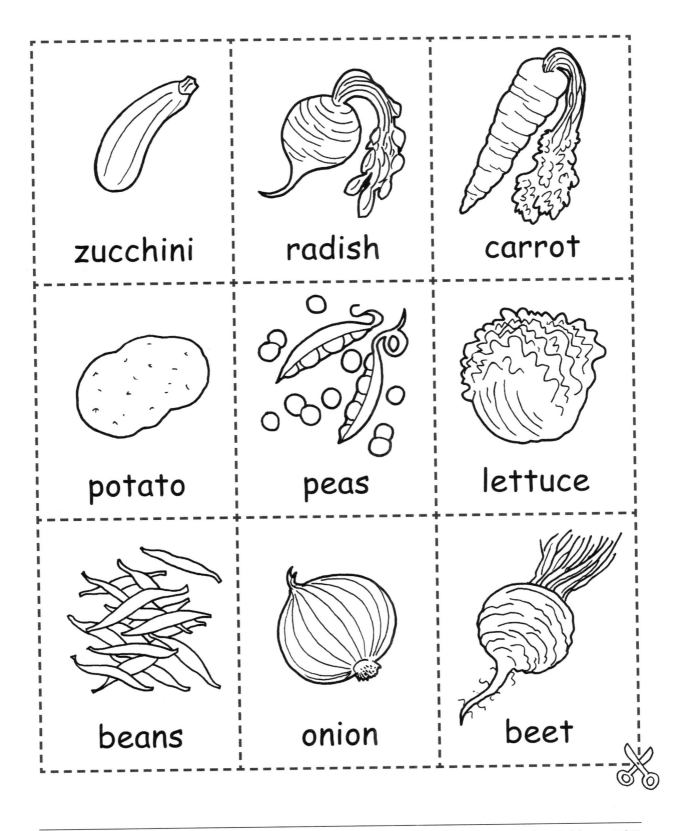

zucchini

radish

carrot

potato

peas

lettuce

beans

onion

beet

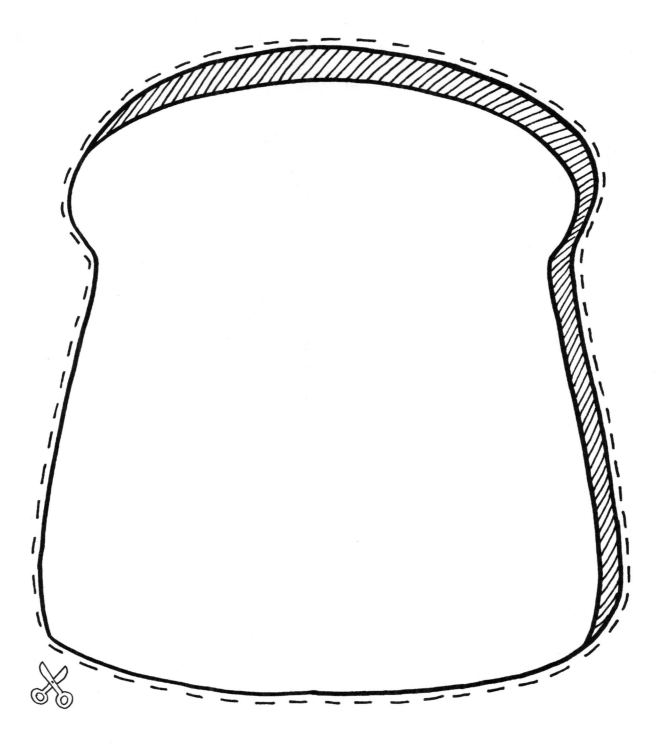

Name _____

We Made Rolls

1. Add 1 tbsp. cinnamon to 1/2 cup sugar.

2. Melt some butter.

3. Open a package of tube rolls.

4. Separate the rolls.

5. Dip the tops in butter.

6. Dip in the sugar.

7. Bake.

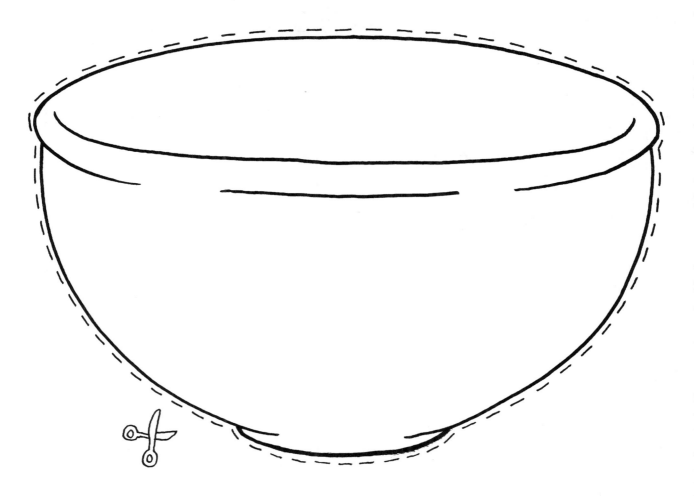

Name _____

My Bedtime Chart

	S	M	T	W	Th	F	S
Put on pajamas							
Wash my face							
Brush my teeth							
Read a book							
Turn out the light